T0321663

MAY THE FARCE BE WITH YOU

Roger Foss

May The Farce
Be With You

OBERON BOOKS

LONDON

First published in 2012 by Oberon Books Ltd
521 Caledonian Road, London N7 9RH
Tel: +44 (0) 20 7607 3637 / Fax: +44 (0) 20 7607 3629
e-mail: info@oberonbooks.com
www.oberonbooks.com

Photograph on page 19: An audience at the Whitehall Theatre watching
Reluctant Heroes; source unknown.
HB ISBN: 978-1-84943-151-4
E ISBN: 978-1-84943-602-1

Contents

1. LOL and the world LOLs with you.......................... 7

2. More Farce Please, We're British 19

3. A Conversation with Cooney.................................. 33

4. The Man Who Made Queen Victoria Giggle........ 57

5. Comedy of Terrors...68

6. Let's Farce the Music 78

7. Spent Farce? 89

8. Fifty Farces to See Before You Die Laughing.........99

Bibliography of sources 115

1. LOL and the world LOLs with you

'Laughter is a noise that comes out of a hole in your face'
– Ken Dodd

IF YOU COULD download theatre from iTunes, where would you put your farce? You'd end up having a genre crisis. Too niche to file under 'Comedy', too mainstream to file under 'Classical', farce doesn't seem to go with a digital mindset. Even so, it's probably only a matter of time before theatre audiences log out of real life and text 'LOL' to each other on smartphones rather than actually laugh out loud. Picture it: a West End theatre packed with rows of emoticon-type smiley faces watching the umpteenth revival of Feydeau's *A Flea in Her Ear*, all madly sending text-speak to each other whenever the actors deliver a LOL moment. Silent comedy? No loud laughter? Unsmiley faces? Tragic.

FWIW (for what it's worth, to non-texters), IMHO (in my humble opinion) the age-old tradition of people coming together to have a good laugh at people doing silly things is too culturally robust to surrender to the lost-in-cyberspace experience. The coupling of farce and laughter is a marriage made long ago in ancient showbiz Heaven: an arrangement that has had its conjugal (and critical) ups and downs, but was probably always destined for a laugh-out-loud ending.

When you trace the history of farce, it was Aristophanes who more than likely led the way with *The Birds*, and so it went on, right up to Basil Fawlty's 'Don't mention the Germans' and *The Thick of It*. But there's always been a genre-slippage to farce, and it has has never been more slippy than in the past hundred years, when elements of farcicality have naturally flip-flopped between stage, film and television.

Even so, many of our major twentieth-century playwrights have adopted or explored farcical forms. Michael Frayn's *Noises Off*, Alan Ayckbourn's *Bedroom Farce*, Joe Orton's *Loot* and *What the Butler Saw*, Peter Shaffer's *Black Comedy*, Alan Bennett's *Habeas Corpus* and Tom Stoppard's *Dirty Linen* are all examples of writers taking the dramatic and the comic possibilities of farce as seriously as tragedy. More recently, a new generation of playwrights has discovered the power of farcicality. *One Man, Two Guvnors*, Richard Bean's English reworking of Goldoni's classic Italian comedy *The Servant of Two Masters*, owes most of its laugh-out-loud quotient to popular comedy forms harking back to the *commedia dell'arte* and traditional elements of farce, such as disguise, mistaken identity and slap-stick. David Harrower's *Government Inspector*, which premiered at the Young Vic in 2011, is another instance of a classic comedy given a broad comedic makeover, by transforming Nikolai Gogol's classic social satire into an insane farcical nightmare.

At the mass consumption end of the spectrum of comedy, the world of the TV sitcom has thrived on farcicality. Watch reruns of *I Love Lucy*, *Keeping Up Appearances*, *Rising Damp*, *Frasier* and *The Office* and you'll discover some humorous complication or other indelibly stamped with farce on the bottom.

John Cleese has acknowledged the influence of French farces on *Fawlty Towers*. The French, whose deep understanding of farce is probably embedded in the Gallic gene pool, are particularly adept at leaping the genre gap between farce onstage and farce on-screen. Jean Poiret's 1973 play *La Cage aux Folles* began life as a stage farce. It then transferred successfully to film, and ended up back on the musical stage, with a book by Harvey Fierstein set to lyrics and music by Jerry Herman. Pierre Barillet and Jean-Pierre Grédy's 1977-set play *Potiche*, with its women's lib theme, is another example of a farcical stage situation working equally well on film in 2011.

From its earliest days, Hollywood comedians begged, borrowed or stole facets of farce they had used in vaudeville or music hall and turned them into silver screen comedy gold. In turn, Mack Sennett, Charlie Chaplin, Laurel and Hardy, The Three Stooges, Abbott and Costello and The Marx Brothers inspired the likes of Jerry Lewis, Billy Wilder and Woody Allen and the screwball capers of Frank Capra and Peter Bogdanovitch.

Nevertheless, farce is on home territory in a theatre full of people laughing out loud at other people onstage coping with unreal situations. From the fantastical farces and double entendres of Aristophanes and the scheming Roman-era slaves and libidinous old codgers of Plautus, to the contemporary domestic worlds of Ayckbourn, with the likes of Shakespeare, Goldoni, Molière, Feydeau, Arthur Wing Pinero, Ben Travers, Ray Cooney, John Chapman and numerous other expert farceurs in between, farce has made us laugh by putting a scalpel to the vices and vanities of flawed characters driven close to disaster by wonky moral satnavs.

But what is farce? American drama critic John Mason Brown once aptly described farce as 'comedy written with a slapstick rather than a pen. Its business is to make us accept the impossible as possible, the deranged as normal, and silliness as a happy substitute for sense.'

According to actor-producer Brian Rix of Whitehall farce fame, the whole point of farce is that it is broad comedy teetering on the edge of tragedy: 'It always threatens ultimate catastrophe, and this is what sustains the dramatic tension,' Rix writes in his autobiography, *Farce About Face*, 'but by a slight twist it makes people roll about with laughter. It is tragedy with its trousers down.' Or as John Mortimer famously describes it in relation to Feydeau's farcical adventures into adultery: 'Tragedy played at a thousand revolutions per minute.'

Actor turned farceur Ray Cooney, who developed his craft as a writer in Rix's Whitehall company, agrees with the tragi-comic connection: 'What I write about as farce could easily be treated as tragedy in other hands. What Shakespeare does with kings, I do with taxi drivers.'

Today, many people would probably sign up to the idea that farce is tightly plotted comedy of bad manners, with protagonists (mostly men, rarely women) caught in potentially disastrous situations (usually in or near the bedroom) and employing split-second exits and entrances (invariably involving lots of door-slamming) that rev-up into a kind of face-saving relay race – low comedy based on human frailties with physical action that almost belongs to a race apart.

But before running away with the idea that farce is simply frantic fun with sexual overtones, as in Feydeau's farces, it's worth remembering that, over the years, farce meant different things at different times.

The French and the Italians first coined the word *farci*, or *farcie*, not in the theatre but in the kitchen and the medieval church. The term is derived from the Latin *farcire*, 'to stuff' meat or other foods. Originally the vernacular 'stuffing' inserted between passages of Latin liturgy or during the more serious parts of seasonal mystery play cycles, by the sixteenth century the 'farce' had evolved in France and in Italy into loose playlets designed to create laughter, often performed by the travelling troupes from which Molière emerged. The farcical influence was felt in puritanical England too, where tomfoolery, buffoonery and clowning had always been a part of medieval and Tudor drama.

By the Restoration, when the word farce was coined in England, it was not generally used to refer to a special type of comic stage technique at all, but to short, crude humorous plays which were becoming popular at the time. In 1667, Samuel Pepys was recording how a farce, *The Feigned Innocence, or, St Martin Marr-All*, made him laugh: 'It is the most entire piece of mirth, a complete farce from one end to the other, that certainly ever was writ. I never laughed so in all my life'.

By the eighteenth and the nineteenth centuries 'comedy' and 'farce' could mean the same thing. The same play might be described as a 'comedy of manners' on one poster, a 'farce' on another. It was common practice to label any short piece opening or closing a bill as a 'farce', even if there was nothing farcical about it. The French constantly got their comedy knickers in a twist describing some farcical comedies as *farce*, but others as *petite comédie* or *précieuses ridicules*.

The *Oxford English Dictionary* definition of farce includes: 'a dramatic work (usually short) which has for its sole object to excite laughter; an interlude.' I'll go with the laughter. At its heart, farce employs its theatrical ingenuity to make people laugh out loud. It's a communal experience. And in good farces you'll always find a subversive side lurking somewhere behind the funnies, whether it's in Joe Orton's *What the Butler Saw* or Ray Cooney's *Run For Your Wife*. As Sir Peter Hall has noted, farce 'allows us to watch the sort of bad behaviour that we could never publicly endorse, but which we secretly know we might be capable of.' But farce's prime purpose is to create characters, situations and action that tickle funny bones – a fun-poking experience that critic Laurence Kitchen, in his book *Drama in the Sixties* calls, rather snootily, 'The pop art of canteens and seaside piers'.

For me, the cathartic experience of crying with laughter at a farce is every bit as potent as sniffling into a Kleenex during a romantic weepie. Laughter is as natural as breathing. We all arrive on the planet crying out loud first and laughing out loud next. Laughter is in the human DNA chain long before we learn to talk and toddle. Comedians die without it. Theatre audiences roll in the aisles doing it. Beauticians claim it loosens facial wrinkles.

Is laughter really all down to a chemical reaction within our pituitary glands? Does it simply rely on beta-endorphins triggering a humorous high? Has it evolved in humans over millions of years, or have the God-fearing creationists got it right when they claim that laughter simply comes direct from the Almighty. 'Let there be laughter'… 'and lo, Adam's Rib was tickled pink.' But then the Old Testament never was known for its jokes.

Lofty thinkers such as Aristotle, Kant, Darwin, Bakhtin and Bergson have pondered deeply on the nature of humour. Joke analyst Sigmund Freud even imagined the id, ego and superego as a sort of Three Stooges of the unconscious. Personally, I've always had trouble swallowing any of the various titter theories put forward by neuropsychologists, anthropologists and sociologists, because nobody has come up with a more definitive account of the true nature of laughter than Ken Dodd: 'Laughter is a noise that comes out of a hole in your face. If it's from anywhere else you are in trouble.'

Unless you are living in a permanently tragic state of the glums, we know from our own experience how that noise from a hole in the face is powerfully contagious, socially beneficial and utterly universal. In a theatre, you can't beat laughing alongside others during those endorphine-rush moments in a farce when the entire house erupts as if a mighty mirthquake is shaking the foundations.

I can pinpoint the light bulb moment when I first discovered the ability of farce to create knockout laughter. This was not a theatre laugh out loud moment, but a television moment at our home in the East End of London during the summer of 1955. I was just turned ten when my hard-up parents scraped enough money together to rent a black and white television receiver. For me, the box-shaped telly in our front room immediately became a window on another world where brightness and laughter reigned; a world that I barely knew existed beyond the greyscale streets of Cockneydom.

The goggle box became my own private giggle box, from out of which came the likes of Richard 'Mr Pastry' Hearne, Charlie Drake and *I Love Lucy*. Here was a ten-year-old's comedy escape route from the very unfunny reality of a large family coping with post-war poverty. I had already discovered a parallel universe of radio fun. But now, through the medium of the telly, I really could immerse myself in other worlds bubbling with laughter: more fun here, I thought, than cheering yourself hoarse when Old Mother Riley films came on the screen at the Saturday morning pictures. At home, watching comedy shows on the flickering screen, I could roll around laughing on the lino, whilst secretly imagining myself being part of the warmth of the mysterious studio audience that you heard but could never see.

Then, one summer evening, I stayed up late to see *Dry Rot*. I had no idea I was watching the live broadcast of Act Two of a rollicking stage farce, written by John Chapman, which had been packing the Whitehall Theatre for nearly a year. Actually, I had no idea that such things as 'farce' or even theatres existed. Apart from the annual trip to the London Palladium pantomime, theatre-going wasn't for the likes of us. So this transmission must have been the first live play I ever saw.

Dry Rot's fast and furious plot revolving around a racehorse swindle and three dubious crooks who are forced to take increasingly desperate measures to avoid being nabbed, sent continuous gales of laughter across the theatre footlights that seemed to woosh though the television screen and into our front room like laughing gas. If only I could be there at the Whitehall to breathe in the roar of that crowd…

This was the moment when the overwhelming atmosphere of people laughing out loud together in a theatre captured my schoolboy imagination. It has never let go. From then on, I've never been able, or willing, to get farce out of my system.

Of course, I did not have a clue that *Dry Rot*, presented by and starring young actor-manager Brian Rix, would go on to run at the Whitehall Theatre for another three years. I had no idea that one of the critics had described its horse-nobbling plot as 'doubtless intended for an audience of donkeys'. All I knew was that, together, a live audience and a team of actors doing the most extraordinary things on a stage could transform an auditorium into a mighty laughter machine. Sadly, *Dry Rot* is rarely revived. Yet to this day, I can still recall the hilarious Act Two tea-pouring scene.

Decades later, I discovered critic Eric Bentley's comment about the liberating experience of farce: 'Shielded by delicious darkness and seated in warm security, we enjoy the privilege of being totally passive while onstage our most treasured unmentionable wishes are fulfilled by the most violently active human beings that ever sprang from the human imagination.' But the perfect description of farce's laughter effect is by Michael Frayn. In his introduction to Volume One of his *Collected Plays*, Frayn sums up precisely how I felt when, as a young teenager, I went with a coach party to see *Simple Spymen* (also written by John Chapman) at the Whitehall Theatre, by then established as the home of British farce: 'You begin to warm to what you're seeing; your warmth warms the people around you; their warmth warms you back; your corporate warmth warms the performers; you all warm to the performers' warmth.'

Worth thinking about next time you are compelled to text a cool LOL?

2. More Farce Please, We're British

'I didn't know you could laugh in the theatre.
I thought it was like going to church.'

A T FIRST GLANCE it's just a black and white photograph of a theatre audience taken more than half a century ago. But look a little closer. Hilarity is written across the face of every single person. Mouths are gaping. Eyes are gleaming. Tears are flowing. Cheeks are glowing. Sides are splitting. Endorphins are rushing.

Nobody is physically rolling around in the aisles. Another click of the shutter might catch them doing just that.

This roaring crowd is perched somewhere up in the Circle at the Whitehall Theatre in the early 1950s, enjoying a farce written by a member of a bright new acting company, Colin Morris, entitled *Reluctant Heroes*, a comedy of military life as lived by a motley crew of National Service recruits.

The uncredited photo appears in *My Farce From My Elbow*, the first of two autobiographies written by actor-manager Brian Rix (now Baron Rix of Whitehall and President of the Royal Mencap Society), who, at the age of 23, produced *Reluctant Heroes* and starred in it too as gormless recruit Gregory. As well as capturing that precise moment in a theatre when an explosion of shared laughter is about to go ballistic, this snapshot has always fascinated me because it evokes the mostly ignored post-war world of popular West End theatre-going.

Sometimes, when I go to the Trafalgar Studios, the former Whitehall, I fancy I can still hear echoes of forgotten laughter. Who were these men and women wearing grey flannel suits, home-knitted cardigans and NHS glasses? I like to think of them as my kind of people, my parents' and grandparents' generation, the often bad-mouthed coach party trade who would rather see broad farces and big-name revues starring the Crazy Gang than the voguish dramas of Christopher Fry, T.S. Eliot and Jean Anouilh playing at that time – or *anything* by Samuel Beckett. These folk wanted to get as far *away* from John Osborne's kitchen sink as possible.

When *Reluctant Heroes* opened on 12 September 1950 farce was a major force for fun in London's Theatreland – a shining example of escapist entertainment after six bleak years of war and another six grey years of austerity. At the Whitehall, laughs weren't on ration. They were providing an antidote to austerity. Rix and company had tuned in to a commonly shared peacetime mood of optimism. Audience, actors and writers were all facing the same way. They had all lived through the war against Hitler. Virtually every family in the country contained someone who was now a rookie National Service sailor, soldier or airman. When the Korean War broke out a few months earlier in June 1950, almost one hundred thousand British servicemen and women were sent to East Asia.

No wonder that the hearty laughter of *Reluctant Heroes* burst a hell of a lot of belly buttons: the barrack-room humour and authentic service lingo of grumbling soldiers chimed with the times. 'It can be recommended with the utmost confidence as one of the most effective tonics now available against depression caused by conflict abroad and strikes and high taxation at home' observed an unnamed *Morning Advertiser* critic. In its own way, *Reluctant Heroes* was as topical and as relevant as Osborne's *Look Back in Anger* six years later.

Elsewhere in London's not-so-glittering West End of 1950, farce was staple fare, rather like musicals are today. At the Strand Theatre, veteran farceurs Robertson Hare and Arthur Riscoe were renewing their 1948 stage partnership in Vernon Sylvaine's hilarious comedy *Will Any Gentleman?*, about a meek and mild chap given a split personality by a music hall hypnotist. *Traveller's Joy*, a farcical door-slamming romp by actor-playwright Arthur Macrae involving an unpaid hotel bill, a divorced couple and an illicit liaison, was doing a roaring trade at the Criterion. *The Dish Ran Away...* by Graham Fraser became a hit at the Vaudeville Theatre, after transferring from the Whitehall to make way for *Reluctant Heroes*. Arthur Wing Pinero's 1911 farce about religious hypocrisy, *Preserving Mr Panmure*, was successfully revived at the Arts Theatre before rapidly switching to the Aldwych Theatre.

The seemingly unstoppable run of *Reluctant Heroes* ended on 24 July 1954 (around about the same time that RADA graduates Joe Orton and his partner Kenneth Halliwell were fancying themselves as budding novelists), but it continued to attract audiences with a UK tour, a film adaptation, and countless subsequent revivals by the network of rep companies up and down the country.

There should be a plaque outside the Whitehall Theatre. For sixteen years under Rix's reign the Whitehall was a national house of hilarity, breaking the Aldwych Theatre team's previous record of ten-and-a-half years of consecutive farces written by Ben Travers. Described by Harold Hobson in *The Times* as 'The greatest master of farce in my theatre-going lifetime', Rix followed his first Whitehall comedy hit with a succession of original crowd-pulling Whitehall farces: *Dry Rot* by John Chapman; *One for the Pot* by Ray Cooney and Tony Hilton; *Simple Spymen* by John Chapman; *Chase Me, Comrade!* by Ray Cooney. Then he took over the Garrick Theatre on and off for nine years and did the same with The Brian Rix Theatre of Laughter.

Forward-looking and fresh, Rix was, I believe, the greatest populariser of farce in the twentieth century. In a shrewd move, he persuaded BBC television to transmit the first act of *Reluctant Heroes* from the Whitehall in May 1952. The result was 'staggering', he recalled in a *Guardian* article published in 2008. 'Even though the play was in its third year there were queues at the box office for months and the BBC's own viewer research

reported that the transmission received the "phenom-
enal [appreciation] figure of 90 out of 100" and that
"there is little to report save tremendous, unqualified
enthusiasm". West End managers now fell over themselves trying to get excerpts on the BBC, while a viewer
wrote: "I didn't know you could laugh in the theatre. I
thought it was like going to church".'

Five months later Rix presented the first full-length
farce live from the Whitehall Theatre – Philip King's
Postman's Knock. It was such a success that the BBC
invited him to produce five more farces each year. There
were more than 80 live transmissions in the 'Brian Rix
Presents' series; the first was *Love in a Mist* by Kenneth
Horne in January 1956; the last was *What the Doctor
Ordered* by Lawrence Huntingdon and Vernon Sylvaine,
broadcast on Whit Monday 1972.

Another early Sixties BBC television series of specially
written 50-minute farces called *Dial Rix* attracted huge
audiences of up to 21 million, with titles such as *Come
Prancing*, *Between the Balance Sheets* and *What a Drag*
by comedy writers such as Ray Cooney, John Chapman,
Kenneth Horne, Tony Hilton and Christopher Bond.

As the star actor in the Whitehall and Garrick
farces, Rix's characters invariably became embroiled
in absurd, seemingly inescapable situations and were
always caught at some hysterical highpoint in the play

dropping their trousers to reveal baggy boxers and a pale pair of legs wrapped in sock suspenders. But it is slovenly theatre history to replicate the idea that Rix was simply a serial trouser-dropper – that the farces he produced and appeared in provided unsophisticated fun while it lasted but ought not now to be taken seriously as comedic theatre.

The mostly youthful Whitehall team aimed to show ordinary post-war working class and middle class audiences a reflection of themselves. Pinero's intellectually respectable turn-of-the-century farces were passé. The silly-ass Travers farces of the Aldwych era had passed their laugh-by date.

Set in the lounge of a *Fawlty Towers*-esque country hotel John Chapman's *Dry Rot* (1954) was a five-star classic, playing for three and a half years at the Whitehall. The plot spins around a pair of flashy loud-suited bookies and their dim-witted sidekick who become embroiled in a horse-nobbling swindle. The comedy chimed with a time when bookie's runners and widely flouted laws against off-course betting were part of the racing scene. Secret rooms, sliding panels and mistaken identities abound in a comic canter that was voted in a 2002 National Theatre poll as one of the 100 best plays of the twentieth century.

Chapman, who went on to write TV sitcoms such as *Fresh Fields* and *The Liver Birds* (with Carla Lane), and the prolific writer-director-producer and all-round farceur Ray Cooney, are shining examples of how fresh new contemporary British farce could capture the affection of the theatregoing public. Yet too often popular stage comedy of this era is either pooh-poohd or completely overlooked.

Rix and his team not only attracted audiences year after year, but also ushered in a flourishing golden age of inventive British farce that linked to the farce conventions of the past but also connected to music hall, variety, *The Goon Show* and *ITMA*, climaxing at one glorious moment in 1983, when Michael Frayn's send-up of the genre, *Noises Off*, and Cooney's ultimate tour-de-farce, *Run For Your Wife*, both began long runs in the West End.

If I wind back to my own theatre-going experience of the Sixties, Seventies and Eighties it's the farces that keep grinning back at me. Naturally, as a boy actor and a drama student, I queued up for the new National Theatre and became infected by the buzz of the Royal Court (where I appeared in Peter Gill's 1967 production of *The Soldier's Fortune* with Sheila Hancock and Arthur Lowe). You got caught up in the excitement of Royal Shakespeare Company seasons, and the buzz of Joan

Littlewood at Stratford East. Rock musicals, like *Hair* and *Godspell*, and the Anthony Newley *Stop the World – I Want to Get Off* phenomenon, were also must-sees.

But while my fellow acting students were enthusing over Peter Brook's *Marat/Sade* or pondering over the meaning of 'Pinter-esque', I was the one with a secret passion for the popular laugh-out-loud Britcoms running in the West End and on tour, the farces that literally ran and ran, like Cooney's brilliantly constructed *Chase Me, Comrade!*, inspired by Rudolf Nureyev's defection to the West. I can still remember laughing helplessly at the surreal visual buffoonery of this piece, especially Brian Rix's eternal victim character morphing through a series of increasingly desperate disguises, including a naval officer, a leaping ballet dancer, a character who stretches to become a ten-foot giant, and a surreal talking tiger-skin rug.

The fake tiger sequence provided one of the most sublimely funny moments I have ever experienced in a theatre, one that also registered at the time with *New Statesman* theatre critic, Ronald Bryden: 'As the animated pelt, a bellowing officer at its heels, scrambles off-stage in a whirlwind of slamming doors, the piece achieves that moment for which the cast, with fingers crossed, nightly hold back: the "take-off", the hysterical consummation when the actors and audience, throwing off restraint and calculation, mutually surrender to the mingled idiocy and ingenuity which is the specific pleasure of farce.'

Once, after an intense morning's rehearsal of *The Soldier's Fortune* at the Royal Court, I sloped off to Shaftesbury Avenue to recharge my humour batteries at a matinee of Terence Frisby's *There's a Girl in My Soup*, by then in its third year in the West End. Maybe it was a yearning for more of that 'mingled idiocy and ingenuity' that drew me there, even it felt like I was embarking on secret laughter-smuggling mission across the Berlin Wall. Coach party farces and anything by Terence Rattigan were just not sexy enough for Sixties swingers. I mean, who in their right mind would plump for the innocent innuendo of *No Sex Please, We're British*, Alistair Foot and Anthony Marriott's hilarious long-runner of the bedroom variety, about a newly-wed couple ordering Scandinavian pornography by mistake, when you could snigger with the in-crowd at the fleshed-out single entendres of *Oh! Calcutta!*

No Sex Please, We're British played in the West End for fourteen years. *Chase Me, Comrade!* ran from 15 July 1964 to 21 May 1966 and was the last of the Whitehall farces. Rix then attempted to run a repertoire of comedies and farces at the Garrick Theatre with members of the old Whitehall team, including ace farce director Wallace Douglas, and featuring comedians such as Leslie Crowther and Dickie Henderson.

The concept floundered financially, so Rix reverted to the tried and tested Whitehall format of presenting (and starring in) single plays for long runs, a strategy that produced some truly fine British farces. Three of them, written by Michael Pertwee – *She's Done It Again* (1969), *Don't Just Lie There, Say Something* (1971), and *A Bit Between the Teeth* (1984) – are funny, clever and inventive plays that easily measure up to anything in the Whitehall output. Yet in decades of theatre-going, I have yet to see any of these plays, or indeed any of the Whitehall farces, given the full professional West End or National Theatre treatment they deserve.

Travers' *Rookery Nook* and *Thark*, King's *See How They Run*, Frayn's *Noises Off* and the some of the well-known Pinero titles are often revived, along with that transgendered dowager from Brazil, *Charley's Aunt*, giving new audiences the chance to glimpse what British farce can do. But why has a work of theatrical genius like *One for the Pot* been ignored? Why overlook an anarchic gem like Pertwee's *She's Done It Again*? These plays, and many other still playable farces from the post-war era, have fallen out of favour. Yet, at the time, Harold Hobson described *She's Done It Again* as 'the funniest in which Brian Rix has ever appeared' and praised its 'delicious and delirious' qualities: 'What looks feeble and hackneyed on the page glows with glorious life in the Garrick Theatre.'

Involving an accident-prone parson, the Reverend Hubert Porter, who becomes embroiled in an increasingly bizarre world of sexual outrageousness and infidelity that leads to a succession of dotty deceptions and mad masquerades, Pertwee pushes a string of Establishment figures to the very brink of moral disaster, at times even echoing Orton's rather more self-consciously outrageous comic salvos against prevailing moral codes in *Loot* and *What the Butler Saw*.

'The libidinous, nervous tax inspector; the Reverend Hubert Porter, terrified of being discovered in his contribution to the great quintuplets deception; the crooked hotel proprietor, nervous, too, because all his machinations go wrong; the dotty old professor Hogg delivering babies by grace and by God – all these characters, and more, in *She's Done It Again*, were threatened by the ultimate catastrophe,' Rix recalls in *Farce About Face*. Similarly, the taxi-driving bigamist in Cooney's much later *Run For Your Wife* (1983) is made to face total disaster once his carefully organised web of deception begins to go cock-eyed and the police start snooping around.

Rix's achievement, apart from dropping his trousers onstage more than any other British actor, like so much good popular theatre, has been virtually forgotten and is rarely included in the familiar narrative that says British theatre in the Fifties and Sixties was all about the English Stage Company, John Osborne, Joan Littlewood and Harold Pinter, with young Mr Orton winking from theatre's naughty step. If there is any critical credit, it is often given with a nod of sage-like condescension. For instance, in his study of 1960s drama, Laurence Kitchen typically claimed that Whitehall-type fare catered for a 'less sophisticated' public. 'These farces are the pop art of canteens and seaside piers.'

No wonder the exceptionally skilled farce writers and actors who emerged from the Whitehall team have never been given their due amongst the post-war new wave of up-and-coming comedy performers and writers such as Frankie Howerd, Peter Sellers, Spike Milligan, Eric Sykes, Frank Muir and Dennis Norden, and Ray Galton and Alan Simpson.

'For some maddening reason our critical friends will always try and find favour with the French variety of farce rather than the English variety,' observed Rix. 'Yet I'll bet we've had a greater number of successes this century than any of your ooh-la-la lot put together. John Chapman, Ray Cooney, Michael Pertwee and Philip King have provided more laughs for more people in the theatre than probably any other bunch of writers in history.'

Cooney is still creating, or revisiting, his cock-eyed characters embroiled in cock-eyed situations. But in theatres where the laughter of farce once hit the rafters – and kept the box offices happy too – you are more likely to hear the sound of musicals.

Still, whenever I look at that black and white photo of a distant crowd laughing at Rix's Whitehall team going full pelt, I like to think of that golden age of British farce and those marvelous comedies that have mostly been consigned to the wheelie bin of theatre history. Inevitably I get a nagging feeling that without those plays, and without the kind of people who created them and laughed at them, our current theatre is missing something rather special.

3. A Conversation with Cooney

'To be in a theatre full of people laughing at what you have taken great pains to create is a fantastic feeling.'

W ITH A CAREER in the theatre spanning more than 65 years, Ray Cooney is Britain's world-class farceur. Who else has spent a lifetime finding ever-ingenious ways to celebrate the farcical foibles of human nature. By my reckoning, he has written, directed, produced and appeared in more stage farces than anyone currently living on the planet. Starting out as a boy actor in 1946, he served an acting apprenticeship playing with various repertory companies before joining the Brian Rix company of farceurs at the Whitehall Theatre in 1956, where he appeared in *Dry Rot* and *Simple Spymen*. It was during this period that his talent for creating laughter first emerged.

As a fan of farce, over the decades I have seen almost all of Ray Cooney's West End productions, and many of those revived in provincial repertory theatres or on tour, from the insanely inventive *One for the Pot* (co-written with Tony Hilton) and the sexually provocative *Not Now Darling*, to *There Goes the Bride, Move Over Mrs Markham* (written with John Chapman), *Chase Me, Comrade!, Wife Begins at Forty, Why Not Stay for Breakfast?, Run For Your Wife, Two into One, Out of Order, It Runs in the Family, Funny Money, Caught in the Net* and its sequel, *Tom, Dick and Harry*.

We sat down and talked about a life spent in the hectic world of headlong humour at the calm-as-a-cucumber Cooney residence in Essex, where his artist wife Linda provided chunky cheese and pickle sandwiches and lashings of hot coffee while I fiddled on the sofa with my recording device.

Funnily enough, I was slightly in awe of meeting someone who has given me so many hours of laughter in the theatre. After all, it was those hilarious Cooney farces at the Whitehall that had such a big influence on my development of a sense of humour in my teens. I've long believed that what Ray Cooney doesn't know about farce is nobody's business, so I nodded sagely as the man the French have described as 'The English Feydeau' fielded my questions in his typically good-humoured, self-effacing manner.

As we talked, I found it hard to believe that Ray Cooney is still keeping the farce flag flying in his eighties. His latest directing project is a film version of his most successful farce, *Run For Your Wife,* starring

Danny Dyer, Neil Morrissey, Denise Van Outen and Kellie Shirley.

Of all the great twentieth-century farceurs, Ray Cooney is the last still standing.

Before we talk about your theatre work, can I ask you about your film adaptation of *Run For Your Wife*? How on earth do you make such an intricately calibrated stage farce work on screen?

Some of my earlier plays were made into movies but they were 95 per cent the play with some location work inserted – basically, the stage play on screen. You couldn't get away with that today. If you're trying to make a genuine movie you need to 'open it up' as they say, although I like to quote the film version of *There's a Girl in My Soup* as an example of opening up a successful stage comedy so much that they kind of lost the thread. Stage farces are generally claustrophobic, so in opening them up you have to be very careful.

Fortunately *Run For Your Wife* was the only play I have written with two sets in one – the home of each wife. John Smith, the bigamist cabbie, spends his time rushing from one to the other, so in a way the plot was already opened up for me and I simply had to fill in the period when he was travelling from one place to the other and get him into various scrapes on the way.

I kept the original story just the same and introduced one other character, but the big change is that the film is set today, not in the 1980s, so obviously you have to introduce things like mobile phones and update some of the language. As for the basic premise that roots the comedy in reality, well, bigamy remains a criminal offence, fortunately for me, though not for a liar like John Smith or his innocent wives!

Looking back on a life in comedy, where did it all begin for you?

All I ever wanted to be was an actor. I never knew why. My mum and dad scrimped and saved to send me to a rather good school, Alleyn's, but I kept saying it's no good getting me marvellously educated because I want to leave as soon as possible and get into the theatre. I think they thought I would grow out of it. But when I reached fourteen we sat down with the headmaster and came to a deal whereby if I could find a theatre job during the summer holiday they would let me go. I don't think anyone ever believed I would get very far. Undaunted, I walked round all the West End agents and finally got an audition for *Song of Norway* at the Palace Theatre – and that was it.

Were you already into comedy, even at that young age?

As an aspiring actor I didn't especially want to do comedy. I thought I would be the next Laurence Olivier. I was always aware of popular comedy. My parents loved variety and couldn't afford a babysitter so they took me along with them to places like the Brixton Empire and we'd go and see great comedians like Max Miller, Sid Field and the Crazy Gang. I was into Abbott and Costello then, and the Bob Hope 'Road' films too, but it was in the variety theatres where I first became aware of the power of laughter and being in an environment where you could get carried away by it.

Do you come from a theatrical family?

Not at all. Dad was a carpenter who had a very jokey personality. Mother worked too, but from the age of sixteen she became a paraplegic after an injury at work. On her first day there she went to sit down and a young office boy played a prank by pulling her chair away. She spent over a year in hospital. For the rest of her life she walked with a stick or was in a wheelchair. She was a fantastic person, very supportive of me.

So when did you first become aware that there was such a thing as a stage farce?

Not until I came out of the Army, after my National Service, when I joined what I thought was going to be a weekly repertory company in Wales, only to find out on the day I arrived at a small village just outside Cardiff that it wasn't quite what I expected. Outside the village hall a poster advertised a list of popular plays, including *Jane Eyre* and *Smiling Through* and the Philip King farce *See How They Run*. What I thought was a six-week season was in fact a different play every night. Without realising it, I had joined the last of the touring fit-up companies. You learned two plays in the first week and by the time I had finished I had a basic repertoire of 40 plays – everything from broad comedies to serious tragedy. People came from miles around to see 'the drama'. I then joined the weekly rep manager Frank H. Fortescue's Famous Players company in Blackburn for 18 months, appearing in a different play every week.

You mention playing in *See How They Run*. At the time were you aware of other farces by writers such as Ben Travers, Pinero or Feydeau?

Not really. When I did *See How They Run* in fit-up it had not long finished its first West End run. But you have to remember that in the early 1950s, to those of us in our twenties, Ben Travers' plays seemed as if they were from another era. To me, *Rookery Nook* was old hat. Of course, I didn't have a clue then that much later on in my career I would get to know Ben and direct one of his plays.

The Brian Rix company at the Whitehall Theatre was the launchpad for your career. How did you first become involved?

Like every rep actor I wanted to get into the West End. While on a break from Blackburn I went with my parents to see *Reluctant Heroes* at the Whitehall. I thought it was so funny that I wrote to Brian telling him how I had a lot of experience and that I thought my comedy talents were quite something. He wrote back and said he was auditioning the next week for a try-out tour of a new farce by John Chapman called *Dry Rot*.

In the meantime I had landed a television job up north at Granada, so I pulled out of the play. The series should have run for twelve weeks but only did six, so I wrote back to Brian and said I'm still available. He rang my mother and asked 'How old does your Raymond play?' She said: 'How old do you want him to play?' Brian explained that it was a spivvy character, and she replied: 'Oh Raymond can be spivvy as well!' And that's how I got the role of Flash Harry on tour, the part played in the West End by Basil Lord.

What led you into writing for the Whitehall company?

Brian asked me to be in the next comedy by John Chapman, *Simple Spymen*, which opened in 1958 and ran for almost four years. During the run I thought I had better do something else during the day except chase girls and play tennis, so I suggested to another actor in the company, Tony Hilton, that we write something as a vehicle for Brian, who hadn't got his next play. We knew that Brian wanted to get away from the goonish North Country character he had become well known for. But on the other hand, we also knew that audiences liked him as that character. So we came up with the idea of having him play the lovable goon as one of identical triplets. In the end Brian played no less than four different characters in *Simple Spymen*, with the assistance of doubles of course. It was probably his most physically demanding farce.

For that first play, as you were honing your writing skills, did you ever work out how the great farceurs of the past constructed their comedies?

Actually, I didn't give them any thought at all! I just sat down with Tony and we wrote. I guess I didn't realise how much I'd soaked up about comedy as an actor in fit-up and weekly rep. I'd been in plays by Ben Travers and Philip King but, to be honest, as a young actor you didn't really appreciate what went into the writing of them. With *One for the Pot* we quickly learned how to fine-tune the plot and make the complications of Brian's various characters popping on and off the stage work because we did three full try-outs of the piece – at Richmond, Birmingham and Wolverhampton. After each trial run we made huge rewrites to polish the comedy and get it absolutely right.

So rewrites are an essential part of the creative process for you?

Yes, I very soon realised that try-outs with audiences are part of the structure of writing farce. With farces, you never get it right first time. After *One for the Pot* the kind of plays I write became very convoluted and almost thriller-like in their construction – in *Run For Your Wife*, a guy tells a lie, and that lie leads to another lie which spreads like a virus. With *Funny Money*, after the first rehearsed play reading in front of an audience, the first act went so wonderfully well that I thought I had an instant hit on my hands. But during the second act I soon discovered that I had actually gone off on a wrong tack in the first act, which meant that nothing worked in the second. I went away and rewrote the entire second act before the next try-out tour went into rehearsals six weeks later. Luckily I hit upon something that did work!

Acting and writing as part of the Whitehall company must have been quite a learning experience.

Yes indeed, though I think a lot of it must have come to me naturally. By the time I joined Brian I had done over one hundred plays as an actor with the fit-up company and in weekly rep. I learned a lot about what works and what doesn't work in farce from being onstage with Brian and from Wallace Douglas, who directed most of the Whitehall farces. Basically, I think the Whitehall success was all about teamwork. I discovered that you really do need a team for broad farce, a group of actors who can work together in rehearsal and onstage in front of the audience, because playing farce is very much like a tennis match. You can't play tennis on your own, you have to ensure you hit the balls to each other properly and you have to do it with perfect timing. That's why you can't have a star actor who thinks the focus is just on him or her. Actually, since Brian, I never wrote with any specific actor in mind.

My own memory is that the Whitehall farces made stars of actors like Basil Lord, Leo Franklyn and Larry Noble. Whatever they got up to onstage, they always remained completely in character and yet they seemed to have a strong bond with the audience.

I suppose that's because Brian assembled a team who had come from the same background as I had, mostly from rep – a breed of actor who knew how to connect with audiences and deal with building the laughs. Let me just say this about Brian Rix: nobody in the past or in the future has ever, or will ever, achieve what he did as an actor-manager at the Whitehall and later at the Garrick. He has never really been given the credit for it. Brian got his knighthood and baronetcy for his work for charity and with Mencap. But what he did for the theatre is totally unique. At the Whitehall he presented only five farces in about 21 years and he starred in each one. Those plays were sold out months in advance. He ran a wonderful ship. It was Brian who had the idea of doing TV excerpts from the Whitehall. Nobody had ever done that before. It will never be done again.

How do you go about creating a farce?

Actually I always thought of my plays as comedies with farcical overtones. A farce to me is a foolish thing, except that I like to think that at their heart is a serious premise. What I look for initially is the plot. What's the story? Is it rooted in real life? Is it believable enough to draw the audience in. In fact, most of my ideas for plays come from real life, from reading the papers. So I don't really look for a 'funny' storyline at all; in fact I look for a potential tragedy.

In *Run For Your Wife* the premise was very tragic – bigamy. Then I needed a bigamist and I needed wives, so I gave him a wife in Streatham and a wife in Wimbledon. Then I thought, what would be his ideal job? I came up with a taxi driver because it meant he could easily schedule sly trips from one home to another. Then I needed to add a threat to his layers of lies and deception, other than the two wives finding him out, so, as bigamy is a criminal offence, I brought in some policemen.

I usually start the actual work by making a hell of a lot of notes on bits of paper which I then stuff into my pockets. When the bits of paper get to about half a ton in weight I think I'd better get on and write it up. It's a bit like a jigsaw puzzle. Although I left school very early, one of the subjects I was always very keen on was algebra, so I guess that's why I'm quite adept at fitting all the bits together.

So you are working out the comic potential as you build on the basic premise?

Yes, but you won't find many gags or direct jokes in my plays. People often say, 'Oh come on Ray you must know a lot of jokes,' but I don't. Any gags come out of the situation, or at least I hope they do, unless you have a character who deliberately tries to be funny for some reason.

Are you saying that the best farces are tragedies?

Somebody once said that farce is real people in unreal situations and comedy is unreal people in a real situation. I'll go along with that. Farce is difficult to dissect. You are twisting reality but you are not jumping out of reality. And, as I said, the reality of the initial premise may not be all that funny at all. A wife caught in a bigamous marriage, if she discovers it, is suffering the worse kind of betrayal. It's not as though the husband's simply having a fling with a girl at the office. He's actually got another family home, another life, pets, children…for a woman to discover all of that after 20 years of marriage is no laughing matter. And *Wife Begins at Forty* deals with the serious issues of midlife crisis for women. So when I'm writing, I might be going down a potentially tragic avenue for a while but the actual comedic bit doesn't usually arrive until I go upstairs to my room in the attic with my bits of paper and start working on the words, the characters and their peculiarities.

As in *One for the Pot*, the peculiarities and the farcical complications that you eventually engineer certainly place heavy demands on the actors.

That's true. With *Two into One*, I'll always remember Michael William saying after he had been rehearsing for about a week, 'My god, the RSC should be brought down here and given a lesson. It's killing me. It's so complicated. I know someone is due to come through a door but I can't follow the plot!'

I guess in performance there is also the central issue of actors having to deal with the big laughs.

In 1983, when *Run For Your Wife* first opened at the Shaftesbury Theatre, Richard Briers, who was playing John Smith, the taxi driver, called me in a panic. 'What am I supposed to do Ray', he said, 'every time I go to open my mouth at this particular point in the play, they laugh some more. I can't stop them!' Can you imagine the packed Shaftesbury Theatre exploding with laughter and Richard having to control it while thinking about when to continue the action. Even experienced actors like Richard ask what they should do while the laughter keeps coming at them. I say you just have to continue 'in the moment'. Sometimes that makes the audience laugh even more! It's about handling the laughs and not being distracted by them.

But what do say to those who regard farces simply as frivolous formulaic laughter machines?

Well, the purpose of farce is to generate laughter – that's all. For me the only formula is the story. I guess if some academic read all of my work they might come up with a theory or discover a theme running through the plays, but I have never sat down and attempted to fit a farce into a formula.

Would you say there are any basic rules for acting in farce?

As a director I always ask the actors to be real onstage but to be aware they are in a comedy. Of course they need a hell of a lot of energy and an ability to time the comedy. Also, in my plays the characters are speaking in ordinary everyday language – only very fast; there are no fancy monologues to hold on to, which means that you haven't got time to enlarge on anything. And you have to deal with any given situation very quickly, which means having a split-second awareness. The audience doesn't notice it, but the geography of the actors onstage is absolutely vital too. If you've got a funny line followed by an exit, it's no good saying the line in the middle of the stage and then walking all the way to the door, so you have to devise ways and means of exiting that make an impact and build the laugh. It's technical stuff, but it works.

And of course the actors need a heck of a lot of energy to get through a performance.

Yes, but laughter is energising in itself. Gales of laughter coming across the footlights is addictive in some way. It's a wonderful feeling when you get that. It's a pleasure to go to the theatre every evening. As a writer and director sitting at the back of the auditorium, to be in a theatre full of people laughing at what you have taken great pains to create is a fantastic feeling. It's the same for the actors. It's incredibly fulfilling when they hear those eruptions of laughter.

Are there rules for directing farce?

There probably are but I don't follow them myself except for telling the actors to relate to each other onstage truthfully. Farce might be fun to watch, but creating fun is a serious business. Actors that work with me know that my own little shortcut for describing how to play farce is 'eyebrows up'. I don't know where I got it from, but it's impossible to say an unpleasant line when you are 'eyebrows up'. If you say, 'I hate you, please get out of the house' with your eyebrows up you can't go wrong. There's something intrinsically funny about 'eyebrows up'. Which is probably why I have so many lines on my forehead. Try it!

Do you prefer writing by yourself or with a partner as you did with John Chapman on *Not Now Darling*, *There Goes the Bride* and *Move Over Mrs Markham*?

Most comedy writing partnerships are sitcom or gag writers. There aren't too many who sit down and write farces together. With John it was a wonderful partnership. In something like 40 years we never had a cross word. Our partnership began when I had an idea for a farce after reading a short newspaper article about a man in Norway taking a lady to court over a mink coat he had given her. I made lots of notes and had just started to plot it out when John phoned out of the blue. He was writing the *Hugh and I* television series, starring Hugh Lloyd and Terry Scott, and was up to his eyes in it with another seven episodes to go, so he asked me if I would like to help him out. I agreed to co-write with John but, in return, asked him to read my new mink coat script. He liked it, worked on it with me, and that's how *Not Now Darling* was created.

We used to sit opposite sides of a table and act out the dialogue, much as I do now when I am writing on my own – I still get totally lost in the world of the characters as I write. John and I wrote four plays together and the only reason we stopped was because he liked writing for television, so he segued down that path and I carried on in theatre.

Sounds like it was a thoroughly enjoyable collaboration.

Well, everything in my work and my life has been fun. I never get up in the morning without thinking how lucky I am to be doing what I do.

Compared with the naughty French, British farces seem to be rather more innocent – sex comedy without the sex maybe. Are you consciously careful to avoid being too explicit?

When I first started writing we were always aware of the Lord Chamberlain's blue pencil. You were only allowed one 'bloody' in a play. You just took censorship for granted and, let's be honest, *One for the Pot* and *Chase Me, Comrade!* are both very unsexy – although we made up for that with *Not Now Darling* in which sex is talked about a lot – and by the time we get to *Two into One* you do actually see them in bed together. In a funny way, although it has now eased up for writers and there are no limits, it has somehow made a lot of comedy very offensive – anything goes these days.

But if there are no limits to what's said in comedy, doesn't that make farce impossible to write?

I'd agree that it has become much more difficult to hit upon a basic premise. Even so, the dubious morality of the powerful and of politicians has always been good for farce and probably always will be. And getting married is still the basic thread of everything that happens outside of our working existence and family and friends. Alan Ayckbourn is still very clever at taking hold of domestic scenes and spinning them out.

New writing is encouraged today, but new writers don't seem to want to write new farces. Has farce gone out fashion?

The comedy writing focus has gone towards television. That's where the talent is now. It is very difficult for the kids who are starting out to forward their careers solely in the theatre. And it's probably much easier to revive classic farces from the past than to sit down and write something completely fresh and original. Most of the farceurs of my generation were also actors who learned to write farces by appearing in them. It's not possible to serve that kind of apprenticeship any more. Perhaps our only hope is that some young director will get a hold of the classic farces or discover and produce some of the rarely performed ones, and maybe a young writer somewhere will see how genuinely funny they still are and that will spark them into trying to do the same and come up with something new.

Maybe so, but I rarely see farce revivals these days that really work as well as they think they do.

Perhaps the danger is that directors and actors start putting farcical comedy in italics. I remember seeing a production of *London Assurance* at the National Theatre a few years ago. The director's approach was to get the actors to step outside of the play and give the audience a wink. You couldn't get involved in it. They wanted to say: 'this is the style', which meant you didn't really care about the characters or the predicaments they were in. Mind you, it didn't seem to worry two-thirds of the audience who were quite happy to laugh at the nudges and the winks and the asides.

Of course you can have a character addressing the audience. But you have to find a way of setting it up. In *Not Now Darling*, Gilbert Bodley has asides that begin when he opens what you think is a just a door, only to reveal a well-stocked cocktail cabinet. He looks at the audience and says: 'No office should be without one,' which establishes that he can make remarks to the audience, now and again but not all the time. It would be a pity to take *One For Your Wife* and have John Smith nudging the audience. It would get plenty of easy laughs but I wouldn't accept it. It's cheapening. Oh well, maybe they'll be sending up my plays in the future!

By the way, thinking of the likes of Gilbert Bodley and John Smith, I wonder why men are invariably the ones caught in farcical predicaments and not women?

Why men? I haven't the faintest idea! Except that it's a very male-dominated existence we all still live in. But in *Move Over Mrs Markham* it is the two ladies who cook up the plot and in *Wife Begins at Forty* the play is kicked off by Linda, the suburban housewife, when she begins to question her seventeen years of marriage. In the film of *Run For Your Wife* I actually think I improved the roles of the two wives.

Having created so much laughter onstage, do you have any theories about what makes people laugh?

I am not really academically driven or theory driven. I never attended any writing or directing classes. I never went to drama school. Comedy came my way and I just assimilated things as I went along. Had I gone on to university I would have written very different plays. All I know is that we are the only animal that has the ability to laugh, even under terrible circumstance. I'm sure that even in the horror of the Holocaust, in those dreadful concentration camps, some prisoners laughed.

I had a letter once from a woman who had been to see *Run For Your Wife* who said that as soon as she realised the play was about a bigamist she wanted to jump up and run out of the auditorium because she had been caught up in a horrendous bigamous marriage herself. She said she wasn't able to escape because she was hemmed in on either side of her seat, but in the end she was so pleased that she'd been forced to stay as she ended up laughing as much as everyone around her.

You have produced Joe Orton's *Loot*. What do you think of Orton's use of farce?

I look at *Loot* and *Entertaining Mr Sloane* and in a way they aren't believable – it's as if Joe didn't really mean it. I think my own comedies are real, with a silly twist to them, whereas with Orton it was always on another darker plane. Very funny, but as if everything is being said in italics.

What do you think of my theory that the post-war period was a golden age of farce?

It certainly was a wonderful period for farce, right the way through to the 1980s. But I suppose fashions come and go. Farce won't die. Somebody will come along at some time or another and get us all rolling in the aisles again. You only have to see some of the productions in the little off-West End theatres to know that the acting and directing talent is out there. Those are the people who I am sure will one day find farce and reinvigorate it.

Run For Your Wife was listed by the National Theatre as one of the top 100 plays of the 20th century. If the National decided to stage a Ray Cooney farce, which one would you like it to be?

Two into One. Set-wise it's more interesting to direct. My wife has just returned from a painting holiday in Italy and they were in a tiny village with a huge ornate theatre where they were doing _Two into One_. But I don't have a favourite. Each play I am working on at any given moment is my favourite.

Have you thought of sitting down and writing your autobiography?

Lots of people have suggested it. I'd much rather be getting on doing something now rather that writing about what happened in the past. Maybe I should do something in diary form, almost as a matter of history.

Any thoughts of a title?

'Would it be funny if…'. That's what actors often say to me during rehearsal, but then they see my face and decide it probably wouldn't be.

4. The Man Who Made Queen Victoria Giggle

'Rediscovery is long overdue.' – Kenneth Tynan

DID QUEEN VICTORIA *ever* laugh? For decades, the widowed Queen presented a funereal face in public. She may not have been amused, but her loyal subjects were happily guffawing behind her ramrod back, especially in theatres. In particular, they enjoyed laughing at farce. And they did so with a force that must have cracked many a whalebone corset.

In Victorian show business farce ranked alongside melodrama in the popularity stakes. As the Industrial Revolution turned into an entire way of life, farce became as bankable as muck and brass. The nineteenth century boom in theatre buildings, catering for increasingly urban and artisan audiences as well as the better-off toffs in the posh seats, combined with the growth of touring companies, fostered the wide-scale performance and mass enjoyment of farce.

Farce was in the air, like sulphurous London fog was in the lungs. Farce appeared on virtually every playbill

alongside such pure theatrical Victoriana as 'comedi-
etta', 'tragedy', 'burletta' and 'burlesque' until at least
the 1870s, by which time farce had rapidly morphed
from mostly one-act or two-act 'cup-and-saucer
comedy' afterpieces to emerge as the main feature.
Most notably the full-length well-crafted 'knife-and-
fork comedy' created by British farceur Sir Arthur Wing
Pinero and French farceur Georges Feydeau (whose
Amour et piano was his first play to be staged in London
in 1883), not forgetting Oscar Wilde's *The Importance
of Being Earnest* (1895) and the single enduring piece
by Brandon Thomas, whose hit comedy, *Charley's Aunt*,
smashed West End box office records in 1892 and has
received countless revivals ever since.

Just like us, late Victorians sat in the dark in theatres
and laughed at contemporary farcical situations and
dubious human behaviour on stages contained within
proscenium frames. Their theatres may have been
gas-lit – many of ours have discarded the box set and
the fourth wall 'prosc arch' – but the comic themes were
timeless: deceiving husbands trying desperately not to
be found out; social upstarts falling flat on their faces;
undignified authority figures with disaster hanging over
their heads; comic servants on the make.

Then, as now, farces did what Basil Fawlty called
'the bleedin' obvious' – they made people laugh; they

cheered people up. Farce allowed Victorian audiences to laugh their way through the social danger zones of the Industrial Revolution, to feel a shared twinge of guilt and embarrassment when respectability goes haywire. As Sir Peter Hall said in a 1996 interview just before his new production of Feydeau's *Occupe-toi d'Amélie* opened in the West End, farce 'allows us to watch the sort of bad behaviour that we could never publicly endorse, but which we secretly know we might be capable of.' Bearing in mind that Victorian moral codes and strict attitudes to sexuality meant that nobody could ever be offended, British farce inevitably steered clear of the scandalous shenanigans that *Belle Époque* French bedroom farces were exploiting with élan and plenty of ooh-la-la beyond the White Cliffs of Dover.

Arthur Wing Pinero was one of the most popular playwrights of the late Victorian era. He wrote 59 plays, including contemporary social dramas and intelligent 'problem plays' such as *The Second Mrs Tanqueray* (1893) and *The Notorious Mrs Ebbsmith* (1895). The vast majority of Pinero's dramatic output is either long forgotten, out of print or rarely revived, unlike his meticulously crafted farces written for the Royal Court Theatre – *The Magistrate* (1885), *The Schoolmistress* (1886), *Dandy Dick* (1887), *The Cabinet Minister* (1890) and *The Amazons* (1893).

Audiences lapped up Pinero's gallery of pillars of the Establishment who are, for one good reason or another, tempted to move beyond their normal dignified social world, only to find themselves committing the most embarrassing indiscretions. *The Magistrate*, influenced by Feydeau's sexy romp *A Little Hotel on the Side*, sees a red-faced metropolitan magistrate embroiled in a naughty night out ending up facing a criminal court appearance. In *Dandy Dick*, the Dean of St Marvell's spends a night in the local prison after placing a bet on a horse to save his crumbling church spire.

According to theatre historian Michael Booth, Pinero's particular achievement in his farces 'was to launch his characters on a series of fast-moving, improbable but not impossible situations without once treading on the censorious playgoer's toes.' At the time, Pinero's farces were not the period-costumed Victoriana that we see today whenever they are given an airing, but bang-up-to-date comedies peeking behind the social camouflage of 'decent' people.

Pinero may have diluted the overtly filthy fun of French farce, but his strong influence on the development of the formal structure of the full-length twentieth-century British farce was later acknowledged by Aldwych farceur Ben Travers, who described in his 1956 autobiography *Vale of Laughter* how the discovery of an old set of Pinero plays had a major effect on his own work.

> I fell upon them with the rapturous excitement of Ben Gunn lighting upon the treasure of Captain Flint. They were not merely plays to read. Each one of them was a guidebook to the technique of stagecraft. I studied them as such, counting and noting the number of speeches and the method of plot and character development. I discovered for myself the real secret of Pinero's mastery, namely his attention to every line and in every scene the importance of climax.
>
> Stagey old museum pieces they may appear today. But the present-day playwright still relies, for many of his most successful effect, on the rules laid down and illustrated by that old master craftsman.

Just as influential on the development of British farce as we now know it was another eminent Victorian master of the rules of the game. John Maddison Morton (1811-1891), once hailed by Kenneth Tynan as 'the founding father of British farce', was creating wildly popular stage farces long before Pinero was born. While some of Pinero's farces have ended up as *Antiques Roadshow* theatre, occasionally wheeled out to reveal how their polished comic values can still shine, Morton's vast store of deftly constructed pre-Pinero rib-ticklers, mostly based on situations that might arise in day-to-day mid-Victorian life, have been consigned to the dusty old world of archivists and academia.

Rarely revived today, his short farces – he wrote around 125 and every top comedy actor of his day appeared in them in theatres across the UK – were invariably performed as afterpieces on a bill or slotted in to the main fare. His plots and themes hit the Victorian funny bone because they were very much *of* the people, usually grounding a gallery of lower-middle-class characters in a familiar domestic reality that invariably goes haywire through a series of misunderstandings, mistaken identities and elaborate plot devices before some semblance of homely normality is eventually restored.

In bidding farewell to the upper-class comfort zone of earlier eighteenth-century farce, Morton took the everyday anxieties of Victorian living and made them funny. Like Pinero, Morton happily helped himself to the theatrical inventions of French farceurs, while leaving out the saucy bits. His hilarious *Box and Cox* (1847), which has strong claims to be the most popular of all Victorian farces (Queen Victoria laughed so much that she saw it performed twice), combines the plots of *Une Chambre pour Deux* (1839), by E.F. Prieur and A. Letorzec, and *Frisette* (1846), by Eugène Labiche and A.

Lefranc, and is subtitled as 'A Romance in Real Life', flagging-up a spoof of contemporary melodrama.

The premise of the comedy in *Box and Cox* is simple: a money-grabbing lodging housekeeper rents the same room to two men, one occupying it by day and one by night, without either's knowing about the other. John Box, a journeyman printer, is hard at work at a newspaper office all night, and doesn't come home till the morning, while James Cox, a journeyman hatter, is busy making hats all day long, and doesn't come home till night. The landlady gets double rent for the room, 'and neither of my lodgers are any the wiser for it'. A basic double-trouble situation is expertly contrived by Morton and developed into a truly farcical screwball comedy of mistaken identities, false assumptions and an ever-thickening tangle of misunderstandings.

Morton's delightful farces have been consigned to the lumber-room of British theatre, not because the plays are no good or dated, but because of the British theatre Establishment's depressingly dismissive attitude towards any popular comedy that exists beyond the 'classic' repertoire.

Morton made Queen Victoria giggle, twice. But his farcical frolics attracted a more broader-based audience for farce than Pinero, Wilde or even *Charley's Aunt*. He poked fun at social conventions. His characters exist in a mundane world that invariably turns into mayhem. His plots start in the commonplace and escalate into the outer limits of absurdity. His actors were required not only to deliver the real stuff of situation-based farce and quick-fire dialogue, but to connect directly with the audience as themselves, often adding funny 'tags' at the end to round off the piece.

Can Morton's plays raise a titter today? Even the titles exude a whiff of gas mantles and greasepaint. Typical Morton-esque shorts such as *Lend Me Five Shillings*, *Catch a Weazel*, *A Most Unwarrantable Intrusion*, *Who's my Husband?*, *Slasher and Crasher*, *Grimshaw, Bagshaw and Bradshaw*, *Wooing One's Wife* and *The Double-Bedded Room*, demand performance skills and disciplined farce techniques which are probably beyond the capability of most contemporary actors and directors.

Believing that a Morton 'rediscovery is long overdue', Kenneth Tynan brought one of Morton's two-handers, *A Most Unwarrantable Intrusion,* to the National Theatre stage in 1968, as part of a triple bill including a play by John Lennon. Even with a crack cast (Gerald James and a young Derek Jacobi), Morton's glorious depiction of comfy middle class Mr Snoozle looking forward to a peaceful day at home without the family and servants but soon finding himself embroiled in an absurdist comedy of menace worthy of Pinter, was given the thumbs down by the critics, which probably put paid to any hope of a Morton revival.

In 2011, the little Orange Tree Theatre in Richmond rediscovered the same play and presented it in a triple bill with *Slasher and Crasher* and *Grimshaw, Bagshaw and Bradshaw*. Staged under the umbrella title *Three Farces*, the production was a resounding success, proving that Morton's humour still works. *The Guardian*'s Michael Billington praised director Henry Bell's production, 'which confirms why the Victorians loved farce: in a society that craved stability, order and harmony, it was a way of exorcising their darkest fears and fantasies.' Sam Marlowe in *The Times* said 'the cast sparkles as they juggle intricate wordplay with manic stage business'.

For me, watching these wholly delightful plays, it wasn't just the comic choreography, the clever stage business, the running jokes, the disciplined acting or the spiralling-out-of-control plots bringing virtual catastrophe to mid-Victorian characters that shattered my funny bone. It was the sudden realisation of Morton's place in a British comedy lineage that makes him a missing link between Shakespeare's comic muse and music hall and the variety sketch comedy of Fred Karno, Charlie Chaplin and Stanley Jefferson (aka Stan Laurel), continuing all the way through to the Whitehall and post-Whitehall farces and connecting up with popular sitcom writers such as Eric Sykes, John Sullivan and Galton and Simpson.

As former RSC literary manager Colin Chambers (who researched and edited the plays for the Orange Tree) says in his programme notes, Morton's distinctively English humour 'points backwards towards the comedy of writers such as Pope, Gay and Arbuthnot and forward towards The Goons, Monty Python and *One Foot in the Grave*'.

In terms of quirky dialogue and the insidious undermining of social norms through farcical humour, 'Morton-esque' isn't many light years away from 'Orton-esque'. The rapid entrances and exits, slamming doors, running gags and increasingly anarchic situations in *Grimshaw, Bagshaw and Bradshaw*, have a direct line to the accumulation of misunderstandings, identity confusions, physical sleights of hand and verbal chicanery in intricately constructed farcical laughter machines such as Philip King's *See How They Run* or in Whitehall farces such as Ray Cooney and Tony Hilton's *One for the Pot* and Cooney and John Chapman's *Chase Me, Comrade!*.

Morton never really laughed all the way to the bank, even though *The New York Times* obituary in 1891 called his *Box and Cox* 'the best farce of the nineteenth century'. When Arthur Sullivan's operetta *Cox and Box*, based on

Morton's bestseller, opened in London in 1869, Morton received no royalties. Ah well, that's show business.

His rumbustious one-act farcical style out of fashion, Morton died virtually penniless in 1891, just two months before Oscar Wilde's *Lady Windermere's Fan* opened at the St James's Theatre in London and one year before the London premiere of *Charley's Aunt*. Morton lived long enough to make Queen Victoria laugh and to see her celebrate her Golden Jubilee. And although Victoria remained in solemn mourning for Prince Albert, maybe somewhere at the back of her mournful mind she could still hear the mirth that *Box and Cox* generated in happier times when she *was* amused.

The Victorians certainly knew how to construct things to last, like Tower Bridge and the Royal Albert Hall. They also knew how to build rock-solid laughter machines, like *Slasher and Crasher* and *Grimshaw, Bagshaw and Bradshaw*. It's just that we rarely get the chance to enjoy them. Until we do, whenever I watch reruns of *Only Fools and Horses* or *Hancock's Half Hour*, or catch up on a Ray Cooney farce, I'll think of John Maddison Morton and how he got there first.

5. Comedy of Terrors

'You do have to go through a quite rigorous hell in the rehearsal room' – Celia Imrie

ANY COMEDIAN WILL tell you that dying is easy, comedy is hard. Any actor will tell you that farce is hard, easy to die in. If the audience laughs, a farce is funny; if they don't laugh, it isn't funny. Simple. Or is it more challenging than that? As stand-up comic turned playwright Richard (*One Man, Two Guvnors*) Bean pointed out in a radio interview, the real aim of farce is not to make the audience *laugh*: 'the objective is to make them *helpless* – and that's an enormous challenge to set yourself.'

For actors performing in farce, that challenge is *ginormous*. Laughs don't just happen – they have to be earned. According to Brian Rix, there were 575 laughs in *Dry Rot* – roughly five a minute. Precisely how many made the Whitehall Theatre audience *helpless* in 1957, we'll never know.

But the art of raising giggles, guffaws, chuckles and belly laughs and bringing the manipulative farce-writer's imaginary world to life involves far more than manic exits and entrances or verbal and physical dexterity. Delivering scatter-gun dialogue, wisecracks, doorslams, knockabout situations, outrageous puns, sexual overtones and Mr Bean-style pratfalls all have to be pieced together, bit by bit, in the rehearsal room.

Comedies of sexual desperation and mistaken beds depend on precision execution. Turning a cleverly plotted, carefully constructed script into a conduit for helpless laughter is a unique performance skill that can never be pitch-imperfect. Actors tell me there's even an art to slamming a door. It takes real expertise to drop your pants on cue.

Even experienced actors find it quite daunting making the transition from the original printed page to a live stage engulfed by a tsunami of laughter. According to Celia Imrie, discussing her role in the 2011 Old Vic revival of *Noises Off*, 'You do have to go through a quite rigorous hell in the rehearsal room. It's kind of like doing a maths exam really, trying to remember where you come in and where you go out. But the dividends pay off when the audience is screaming with laughter. It's like an injection. Like being in a football team and scoring a goal and when you do it's heaven.'

David Haig, who I regard as one of the few contemporary actors who were born to play farce, told *The*

Guardian's Mark Lawson how the sound of helpless hysteria has its dangers: 'It is a great buzz. But you have to be careful. You can get very precious about where a particular laugh is and whether you get it. It's very bizarre, the way that very minute inflection or intonation can completely destroy a laugh. And you can get obsessed by that one laugh and not be aware that other parts of the play are becoming funnier.'

As Alan Ayckbourn has said: 'Farce needs total expertise. Anyone who uses the phrase "just a farce" is very wrong. Everyone knows if a farce is working or not – are we laughing or are we not? If not, well you've blown it mate!'

Looking back to my own acting career, I confess I once blew it in a farce – big time!

Not Now Darling became an international hit for Ray Cooney and John Chapman in 1968, with ace farceurs Bernard Cribbins and Donald Sinden heading the cast. By 1971 rep theatres across the UK were doing it too ('Direct from London's West End'). I look back in embarrassment to the time when I was cast in the Bernard Cribbins role in a rep production at Worthing's Connaught Theatre – and died the proverbial death.

I had queued at the Strand Theatre to see the original West End production of *Not Now Darling*, a farcical tour de force in which Gilbert Bodley (Sinden), the womanising director of an elegant fur salon, and his prim co-director Arnold Crouch (Cribbins), become uproariously embroiled in the consequences of Gilbert's attempted infidelity. The farce-rich cast, directed by Patrick Cargill, completely nailed a sex comedy that's ultra-slick, wickedly cynical and dripping with punch-lines, half-naked girls hiding in cocktail cabinets, verbal buffoonery and running gags, such as bits of lingerie thrown out of windows. The audience choked with mirth.

Rather like Helen Marsh, the 'I Can Do That' woman in *The Catherine Tate Show*, I thought I could do a Cribbins. Being cock-sure and young, I wasn't prepared to admit that I didn't possess much of Ayckbourn's 'total expertise'. And maybe because we were all comparatively inexperienced actors at Worthing we simply assumed that we could choke the audience into laughing. In the end, we didn't nail the play, we hammered it so hard that nobody out front dared laugh. Well, maybe they smiled loudly, but only out of sympathy. In fact it was so bad on the opening night, even the ushers seemed poised to walk out.

What went wrong? During the first week of rehearsal the company committed the cardinal error of thinking everything was funny and falling about. But by the first night, all those knife-edge situations and running gags that we had worked on and that I knew had produced massive explosions of laughter in the West End were played out in a kind of respectful silence. When that happens onstage you panic internally, but externally you try to carry on regardless, which in itself becomes farcical. I mean, have you ever seen *Noises Off*?

It felt as if we were in a comedy of terrors. We knew our lines. We performed the play word perfect. But we didn't have the technical skills, or the balls I guess, to bounce the comedy without rib-nudging the audience. Maybe we assumed that farce simply involved actors running in and out, dropping their trousers or knickers and slamming a few doors. Perhaps the characters were too overdone – or underdone – to appear truthful. Our comedy timing probably went awry. Some of us thought our director wasn't geared up enough.

My own theory is that we simply didn't know what we were doing and ended up underestimating the intelligence of the audience. Decades later, I still get flashbacks to that most farcical of performances. I've had nothing but total respect for that rare breed of actors – and directors of course – who are able to make a go of farce ever since.

Everybody says that the successful presentation of a farce requires lots of hard graft. But what does the graft entail? Drama schools may well teach farce, but young actors rarely ever see a farce performed, never mind have an opportunity to act in one. Acting in farce demands a level of commitment and experience that is almost impossible to come by these days. Academic theories of farce abound, but you won't find an Idiot's Guide to performing farce.

Even so, taking my cue from Richard Bean, here are my own thoughts for actors on making an audience fall about *helplessly* – a sort of 'Seven Pillars of Norman Wisdom'.

1. Never think you are funny. Never try to be funny. Never nudge the audience. Keep a straight face, even when hilarious things are occurring all around you onstage. As Joe Orton once said, 'farce requires complete seriousness of treatment by the actors and an emphasis on action: there are few memorable *lines* in Feydeau or Travers'. Orton claimed to be a great admirer of Ben Travers who, in a tribute to popular Aldwych farce actor Ralph Lynn, observed: 'Nobody ever appreciated as well as Lynn how intensely serious is the job of being funny.' Ben Travers' own motto at the Aldwych was 'never try to be funny.' Think Buster Keaton on the big screen.

2. Be truthful. Characters, even comic clergymen and conniving bigamists, have to be true to be funny. It is essential for the actor to get inside the character, convince the audience, even if their truthfulness means they are slightly bonkers

and not quite real and even if the predicaments they are in are out of the ordinary. Think Basil Fawlty. Geraldine McEwan, who appeared in the original (disastrous) production of Orton's *Loot*, has described how the farce actor has to feel everything 'much more passionately' than in a comedy, even if the characters are only skin deep: 'Like a good caricature, which catches the essentials of personality but hasn't the complexity of a true portrait.' Think James Corden as Francis Henshall in *One Man, Two Guvnors*.

3. Treasure teamwork. In farce, you can't have a selfish or a starry actor pulling attention at the wrong moment, especially when you are dealing with physical comedy, machine-gun dialogue, outrageous plot twists and complicated stage business. The team counts for everything in farce. Actors need each other more than in any other genre. The great British farceurs achieved their success through teamwork, often writing for trusted actors they knew well. In the 1880s, Pinero's farces were performed by regulars at the Royal Court Theatre; a more or less permanent company performed Ben Travers' farces at the Aldwych in the 1920s, led by Tom Walls, Ralph Lynn and Robertson Hare; Brian Rix's spirited semi-permanent team at the Whitehall worked so well together that they created a style of their own. These days it would no doubt be called an acting ensemble. There are very few of them about.

4. All the vital work is done in the rehearsal room, but the seriously funny work begins onstage when an acting team draws the audience in with them. Remember the devil is not in the gags but in the situation. Play the situation for all its mirth and the gags will fall into place. Don't walk over the laughs. Anticipate the small ripples and the big waves of laughter that arise every night but be prepared for audiences to react differently in each performance. Listen to the play. Listen to the laughs.

5. Rewrites come with the territory. Classic farces are preserved in a kind of theatrical aspic. If they are to have any laughter value, brand-new farces need to evolve organically, often painfully. Joe Orton's *Loot* and *What the Butler Saw* underwent substantial changes before they became revered classics. Actors should be prepared to relearn pages of new dialogue or even an entire act and be ready to change physical stage business if it isn't getting the laughs.

6. Physical dexterity is equal to the verbal agility required in farce. Actors need to be gym-fit to accomplish the physical consequences of the plot. To negotiate Feydeau's ludicrous entanglements, the actors go through a complete body workout. In a typical Ray Cooney or Brian Rix farce, the actors are required to cope with props and objects that take on a life of their own, being bundled in and out of rooms or cupboards, juggling with multiple entrances exits and, more

than likely, going through several character transformations – and all at a galloping pace.

It was this progression to wild physical virtuosity which so impressed theatre critic Benedict Nightingale when Rix played an innocent Parliamentary Under-Secretary to an unfaithful government Minister in Michael Pertwee's 1972 farce *Don't Just Lie There, Say Something* (the cast included a very young Joanna Lumley): 'Tell one tiny lie, and, before you know it, the need for consistency has forced you to pass off your brother as an Australian millionaire, hide your wife and mistress in the cocktail cabinet, slip dope into a policeman's beer, and dress yourself up as a charwoman, probably forgetting to take off your false moustache in your panic.' Phew!

7. Learn the art of timing: when to throw a line away; how to build several laughs on top of each other; how to hold up a scene to allow a big laugh to take its course; how to time an entrance or exit; how reactions generate laughter; how to carry on regardless when nobody laughs.

Is being seriously funny worth all the hard graft? Before he retired from the theatre in 1977, Brian Rix, one of the most successful farce actors that Britain has produced, told journalist Lynda Lee-Potter why it is: 'I really do savour the pleasure of timing a line perfectly. It's rather like changing gear properly or playing a good stroke at cricket, and of course there's the sexual element. It's like making love really well. It's a deeply physical feeling. But then laughter itself is deeply physical – it involves an explosion of energy that can hit you like a sledgehammer in the theatre. A responsive audience whips you so it hurts.'

6. Let's Farce the Music

'If you really want to make an audience laugh, it's the situation.' – Stephen Sondheim

A FUNNY THING HAPPENED on the way home from the theatre. I tore up my Frankie Howerd fan club card. Reprising the role of the devious Roman slave Pseudolus in *A Funny Thing Happened on the Way to the Forum* seemed a good idea at the time, but Frankie's performance turned out to be virtually titterless. For a devoted Frank-ophile, and also a devotee of a musical that is also one of the fastest, funniest farces ever to have been written, this was no laughing matter.

I first became aware of Frankie Howerd when he was the popular star of the BBC's *Variety Bandbox* ('presenting the people of variety to a variety of people'), his trademark catchphrases such as 'Not on your Nellie!' and 'I was am-*aaaazed!*' spluttering out of the radio every fortnight. I joined the Howerd crowd decades before geeky university students wore tee shirts emblazoned with 'Get Your Titters Out!'. But in 1986 a peculiar thing happened. Frankie went to Chichester and I went off Frankie.

With the best years of his comedy career behind him, and playing too much on his leering Lurcio persona in *Up Pompeii!*, here was my all-time favourite stand-up starring in a revival of the musical in which he had triumphed in the 1960s, but instead of an evening of killer laughter and riotous vaudevillian naughtiness he practically murdered the role of 'the lyingest, cheatingest, sloppiest slave in all Rome'.

Far from fit and approaching his seventies, with those lugubrious features described by critic Irving Wardle at the time as 'resembling a half-melted waxen effigy of Edith Sitwell', Frankie gave us the sloppiest Pseudolus in all of Chichester. He was so jaded that he had to sit down for the big musical numbers and sometimes even wandered off the vast Chichester Festival Theatre stage altogether, apparently hoping the audience wouldn't notice. When the production transferred to the West End's Piccadilly Theatre, it lasted just 49 performances.

It was impossible not to feel a great wave of sympathy for an ageing comedian at a part of his life beset by professional setbacks, physical ailments and probably far too many large brandies. Old clowns are always sad figures. But I still wanted to give Frankie a kick up the farce.

What ultimately fascinated me about this dismal experience was how farcical comedy can only truly work its manic magic on the audience when the energy levels onstage are maintained at the correct kilowattage. With songs or without them, farce needs a straight face, clever timing, precision acting techniques and a well-orchestrated pace if the audience is to be carried along on its comedic journey into anarchy and then further and further on into the realms of hysteria.

With the energy onstage switched on at the right level, *A Funny Thing...* does all of these things – script, music and lyrics totally in tune with just about every aspect of farcicality. Get that mix wrong, and the farce switches off.

A Funny Thing... is a throwback to the deepest roots of farce, combining the two thousand-year-old lowbrow comedies of the Roman playwright Plautus with the even lower-brow energy of vaudeville and variety, all jollied along by Stephen Sondheim's perfectly pitched songs. The result is a non-stop laugh-a-thon in which Pseudolus struggles to win the hand of a glamorous but dim-witted courtesan (Philia) for his young master (the equally dim-witted Hero), in exchange for his freedom.

In his biography *Laughing Matters*, co-writer Larry Gelbart describes how he, co-writer Burt Shevelove and Sondheim achieved the perfect music-comedy balance only because they wrote, re-wrote, re-re-wrote, pulled apart and slotted back together, before eventually coming up with the final version. Sondheim too has explained how he resisted the temptation to force jokey rhymes into his lyrics, partly because of their lack of sing-ability but mainly because they don't add to the overall humour of the show. 'I learned from Burt Shevelove (particularly Burt, and also Oscar Hammerstein) that the idea is more important than the cleverness, and that, if you really want to make an audience laugh, it's the situation'.

Crucially for farce, the songs in *A Funny Thing...* never threaten to hold up the situations but tend to suspend the audience and keep them in comic mode, while providing a chance to cool down the laugh-ter muscles. 'Comedy Tonight' ('Something familiar/ Something peculiar... Old situations/New complica-tions...') sets a tone that continues throughout the entire score, with other comic numbers such as 'Everybody Ought to Have a Maid', 'Lovely' and 'I'm Calm' not only supplying a breathing space between dialogue scenes but also nudging the plot along.

When these stage antics transferred to the big screen in 1966, director Richard Lester discarded both its farci-cality and most of its musicality. Lester kept Broadway star Zero Mostel in the lead and brought in comedy veterans Phil Silvers and Buster Keaton and dumped some of the songs, filmed the action on location, adding lots of then-fashionable *A Hard Day's Night* cinematic tricksy-ness, and ended up with 'something peculiar' – and that's despite having skilled British stage farceur Michael Pertwee in the writing team.

When it comes to musicalising low comedy, Mel Brooks (with co-author Tom Meehan) undoubtedly pulled a farce one by adapting his first film, *The Producers*, for the stage and writing a brilliant new score to match his sleazy satire about a dubious Broadway producer deliberately staging the ultimate atrocious-taste musical disaster (*Springtime for Hitler*) that accidentally becomes box office gold.

Like 'Comedy Tonight' in *A Funny Thing...*, the first two numbers of *The Producers*, 'Opening Night' and 'The King of Broadway', establish the comic atmospherics and give the audience a whiff of the brazen and bawdy burlesque business about to follow, when unscrupulous producer Max Bialystock and nervy accountant Leo Bloom scheme to defraud elderly backers to invest in a show that is a dead-cert flop, thereby enabling them to slip off with the loot. *Springtime for Hitler* becomes a surprise money-spinner but the two are sent to jail where they produce another show with the convicts, *Prisoners of Love*, which also becomes a hit and sets them on the road to slightly more honest fame and fortune on Broadway.

With its accelerating pace of action and an accumulation of near disasters that befall Max and Leo, *The Producers* is a prime example of farce and musicality meshed together. There's a kind of seamless linkage between the comedy and the big brash Broadway-style numbers – a chorus girl dressed in giant pretzels; a line of old ladies doing a tap routine with Zimmer frames; a chorus of tap-dancing Nazis in *Springtime for Hitler* – so that the entire intricately constructed comedy edifice comes alive even better onstage than it did first time round on the big screen, partly because the theatre audience is complicit in Max's sleazy moral universe through communal laughter. As theatre critic Mark Shenton shrewdly observed in *The Stage* newspaper, Brooks's stage version is 'a valentine to the art of making theatre itself'.

Brooks himself clearly knew that creating farcical situations and big laughs on a theatrical scale involved more than just slotting in the gags and mad situations around the songs, but required numerous rewrites and revisions, as he revealed in an interview with *Esquire* magazine: 'You build a wall of comedy one brick at a time. If something doesn't work, you've got to dismantle the wall and start all over again to make sure the bricks are interfacing and that they architecturally support the idea. The premise has to be solid or the comedy isn't going to work. When something isn't working in Act Two, sometimes you have to go back to a reference in Act One that wasn't developed clearly enough to get the explosion you want later on.'

Lend Me A Tenor, The Musical, Peter Sham and Brad Carroll's musicalisation of Ken Ludwig's 1986 madcap backstage farce *Lend Me A Tenor,* underwent numerous rewrites and workshops after premiering at the Utah Shakespeare Festival in 2007 and before its short West End run in 2011. Their musical adaptation sticks to the premise of Ludwig's original cleverly constructed comedy about the zaniness that ensues when the world's greatest tenor comes to a small Midwestern cultural backwater to save its opera company by singing Verdi's *Otello.*

The original play's farce structure is as solid as Brooks's wall of laughter – screwball situations involving multiple mistaken identities and an opera house full of mishaps are as furiously paced as anything by Feydeau or Ray Cooney.

But if the potentially explosive comedic value of the musical version loses its firepower in places it's precisely because, unlike *A Funny Thing…* and *The Producers,* the songs and big production numbers throw a jarring brake on the farcical machinery. Just when the opera house mayhem is about to spin out of control, along comes another tap routine or love interest ballad to halt the spiralling action. It's as if, when rearranging the original script, the co-authors ignored a key rule of farce – however absurd the characters and the situations may be, they must be entirely believable within the crazed logic of the plot.

If *La Cage aux Folles* sticks glue-like to the crazed logic of the plot it's probably because book writer Harvey Fierstein and composer Jerry Herman based the musical on the original 1973 gender-bending French stage farce by actor, director and screenwriter Jean Poiret, who co-starred in the hit play when it premiered in Paris in 1973 and also scripted the 1978 film adaptation (which was followed by two mildly funny sequels, *La Cage aux Folles 2* and *La Cage aux Folles 3: The Wedding* and a Hollywood remake, *The Birdcage*, which was so unfunny it turned laughter into an instrument of torture).

The original production of *La Cage aux Folles* enjoyed a four-year run on Broadway and a short season in London in 1986, by which time the story of Albin and Georges, two middle-aged homosexual lovers who run a transvestite nightclub in St Tropez, didn't quite chime with the Aids-panicking times. The escalating plot revolves around the entanglements that develop when Georges' son announces that he is getting married to the daughter of a local morality crusader. Herman's sublime score ('A Little More Mascara', 'The Best of Times', the anthemic 'I Am What I Am') gives the comedy line pause for breath, but continues to illuminate characters and their situations.

We had to wait until 2008 to discover and enjoy the full farcical force of this musical. As critic Eric Bentley observed in *The Psychology of Farce,* danger is omnipresent in all good farce – 'One touch, we feel, and we shall be sent spinning into outer space.' Playwright/director Terry Johnson's small-scale Menier Chocolate Factory production (which later successfully transferred to the West End and Broadway), spun the audience right into the show's sexual danger zone because his production delivered both the language of musical theatre and the language of farce in equal measure, always pushing the 'normality' of life in a St Tropez drag club further and further towards absurdity and culminating in effeminate Albin's farcical attempt to disguise himself as 'mother' when his lover's son brings home his fiancée's ultra-conservative parents to meet them.

The worlds of farce and musical theatre have linked hands ever since Aristophanes used a Greek chorus of frisky frogs to debate the merits of plays by Aeschylus and Euripides. If Richard Rodgers and Lorenz Hart were around in Shakespeare's day, I wouldn't mind betting the Bard himself would have commissioned them to set *The Comedy of Errors* to music and call it *The Boys from Syracuse*. Mozart knew a thing or two about classic farcical plots too. *The Marriage of Figaro* and *Così fan tutti* are farces to the core.

Apart from farce and melodrama, one of the mainstays of Victorian theatre was the burletta – musical farces in three acts with five songs in each. Long before he teamed up with W.S. Gilbert, Sir Arthur Sullivan wrote the score for *Cox and Box or, The Long-Lost Brothers* based on John Maddison Morton's popular mid-Victorian farce *Box and Cox*. In 1948, *Where's Charley?* Frank Loesser and George Abbott's adaptation of Brandon Thomas' classic Victorian college farce *Charley's Aunt* made 'Once in Love With Amy' a hit for Norman Wisdom.

More recently, it was fascinating to see how big West End and Broadway musical comedies, such as *Betty Blue Eyes* and *Legally Blonde* include hilarious moments where farce-like comedy and music are both singing from the same song sheet. In *Betty Blue Eyes*, a musical adaptation of Alan Bennett's film *A Private Function*, the 'Pig No Pig' number suddenly switches the entire show into farcical misunderstanding mode when the aged mother-in-law thinks that she's about to be killed and eaten, not Betty the pig.

In *Legally Blonde, The Musical*, the riotous no-holds-barred second act courtroom scene becomes a killer mini farce-within-a-musical, wittily choreographed around 'There! Right There!', an elaborate production number with the entire cast onstage asking of the witness for the prosecution: 'Is he gay or European?'

There are other times, however, when grafting farce onto music or music onto farce is best avoided, especially when it results in a horrible hybrid like *Popkiss*, David Heneker and John Addison's short-lived 1972 adaptation of the Ben Travers' most celebrated farce, *Rookery Nook*. The songs were reasonably hummable but the farcical comedy that sparkles in the original play was rendered by them, as Frankie Howerd used to say, 'titterless'.

7. Spent Farce?

'One must shake an audience out of its expectations'
– Joe Orton

WHAT IS IT with the British and farce? Take this book. I tell someone it's about 'theatre' and eyes light up as if we're both on an equal intellectual wavelength, somewhere between Radio 4 and *The Guardian*. If I then explain that it's a book about farce, the eyes invariably screw up in a kind of sniffy cringe, as if I'm one of those uncultured types who have their iPod at full blast on a bus while reading *The Sun*.

On the other hand, that same person would more than likely describe how they fell about laughing at *One Man, Two Guvnors*, the heavily farce-influenced comedy that went from the National Theatre to the West End and ended up on Broadway complete with raves from *The Guardian* ('one of the funniest productions in the National Theatre's history') and *The Sun*.

There is another, more frequent response: mention the f-word to non-regular theatregoers and you get a blank stare. Or, 'Oh, you mean the *Carry On* films?'.

Or someone said: 'What, like *Gavin and Stacey*?'. Not surprising really, considering that stage farce doesn't come within most people's radar these days. Look up British Comedy on Wikipedia and you'll find links to everything from Ealing Comedies and *ITMA* to *Beyond Our Ken* and *Smack the Pony*. Farce doesn't get a look-in. But then neither does any stage comedy. No wonder entire generations have grown up to think of theatres as comedy deserts.

As a genre, farce has always tended to straddle popular approval by the mass of theatregoers and snooty disdain by the intelligentsia. It goes with the territory. If a crowd-puller like Plautus occasionally got the thumbs down from the cultural elite in Ancient Rome, then so did the great modern farceurs like Brian Rix and Ray Cooney, whose work at the Whitehall Theatre and beyond has been relentlessly stereotyped as synonymous with everything that's crude, old-fashioned and politically incorrect.

Farce, and popular British entertainment in general, often undergoes one of its periodic 'rediscoveries' by people who see themselves as cultured, or by arts journalists who've probably never actually seen a farce, usually whenever plays by the likes of Orton, Ayckbourn, Feydeau, Pinero or Travers are revived. You've got to laugh. I remember being surrounded by rows of Radio 4 *Front Row* types splitting their sides at Mark Rylance in the 2007 revival of *Boeing-Boeing* at the Comedy Theatre, who wouldn't have been seen dead guffawing at the original production at the Apollo Theatre in the Sixties, at a time when Orton was taking farce conventions to another level of artistry and Peter Shaffer's *Black Comedy* and John Mortimer's version of *A Flea in Her Ear* were National Theatre sensations.

Is it simply snobbery or good old cultural elitism that has driven so many perfectly decent Anglo-Saxon farces into a cul-de-sac called mindless, or simply a question of different types of audiences, as Simon Trussler suggested in a 1966 *Plays and Players* magazine survey of a perceived farce renaissance at that time: 'The intelligentsia, self-created or otherwise, may understand *Loot* because they share its moral assumptions – but they will only go to the Whitehall as a quaint relic of modish pop culture. The staple Whitehall audience, on the other hand, will ignore fashion, either ignore *Loot* or hate it, and not even try to book for *Black Comedy*, through a total identification of the National Theatre with an exclusive sort of highbrow art.'

Half a century later, highbrow attitudes to farce haven't changed all that much, except that those lowbrows and no-brows who still identify theatre in general with narrow exclusivity probably prefer to go out to see blockbuster musicals or stay at home and laugh at *Mrs Brown's Boys* or *Benidorm* on TV, while the intelligentsia convince themselves that it's cool to go raking through the quaint relics of popular live theatre and claim them as their own in broad comedies like *One Man, Two Guvnors*.

Amidst all of this, farce finds itself in a funny position. The word farce appears in newspaper headlines almost daily, usually to describe the latest political farrago or, more often than not, as a euphemism for an almighty cock-up. But, ironically, although the word farce might be in common media usage, it is not an integral part of the common everyday language of theatre that it was up to only a few decades ago when farces were a mainstay of the West End and regularly performed by rep companies and touring outfits or pulling in the crowds for entire summer seasons.

For fans of farce, this is curious. In a world where sex is on everybody's lips and when the headlines are all about the rich, the powerful and the respectable up to their necks in blatant political corruption, you might have imagined that an up-to-speed contemporary farce would be the perfect medium to get us through hard times. As *The Times* critic Irving Wardle once said: 'The miracle of farce is that it represents a spectacle of human greed, cruelty and lies which sends you out of the theatre feeling the world is a good place'. Or should we just leave it to the improv mockers on *Mock the Week*.

So is a centuries-old genre in danger of petering out, or at least becoming a kind of dotty elderly relation of theatre? The main thing about stage farce today is that nobody writes them. Well, certainly not like they used to write them in the past. Naturally, broad comedies and light comedies regularly come and go, but a major production of an entirely original farce is as rare as a frog in a crinoline.

Shakespeare's *The Comedy of Errors*, Frayn's *Noises Off* and major productions of the obvious output of Orton, Wilde or Ayckbourn are in a narrow band of regular farce revivals, with the odd Pinero or Travers popping up from time to time. The classic crowd-pleasers were never written with posterity in mind. If they have become classics it's not just because they are funny costume plays from another era, but because the flawed human frailties they depict are timeless. Yet the one theatrical genre that thrives on tapping into the taboos of our time has itself become a little bit taboo. I mean, where can you find the successors to Travers, Cooney, Orton and Ayckbourn?

New writing schemes have produced some brilliant playwrights, who use theatre to explore the challenges of contemporary life in interesting and challenging ways. Yet farce, with its requirement for digging beneath surface reality in a comedic way to reveal our hidden urges, is a no-go zone.

You can see why new, even established, playwrights may prefer to take a different path to comedy fame and fortune and transfer their farcical impulses to other media. Creating a stage farce from scratch is daunting. Apart from the technical demands in terms of plotting, pace, character development, comic business, situation (and just being downright funny), the ability to rewrite again and again until the clockwork ticks along nicely is essential – and that can be scary.

Even a highly experienced actor/sit-com writer like Peter Tilbury (*Birds of a Feather, Chef!*) took fright when writing his own original French bedroom farce, *Under the Doctor*, which received its West End premiere in 2001. 'Farce is a huge comic challenge,' he said just before opening night. 'Comic construction is fascinating and farce is the most cleverly constructed of all comedies. It's more difficult than anything I've had to write and took far longer. It makes me wake in a cold sweat in the middle of the night with "Oh my God, that bit doesn't make sense".'

As it turned out, Tilbury's play didn't make enough sense to the audience to get them laughing much beyond the opening night. Paul Taylor of *The Independent* said:

'The material lacks the momentum and remorseless logic that would allow Fiona Laird's production to take off into delirium. A farce that doesn't make you helpless with laughter is one in need of help.' *Under the Doctor* may have needed emergency treatment, but at least Tilbury was brave enough to give farce his best shot.

To bring about Taylor's 'helpless laughter', every single moment of a farce has to work. But nowadays there is no farce infrastructure within British theatre where novice farceurs – writers, directors, actors, designers and producers – can work together as a team, or try out ideas with audiences in order to bring a play up to the required level of precision. There is no farce equivalent to the stand-up circuit, or the flourishing off-West End venues where forgotten musicals are lovingly revisited. Farces don't just emerge from one person's head. In the days when the Aldwych and the Whitehall echoed with laughter, the writing and rehearsal process was made easier because there was a continuity of cast and production from one show to the next. Timing and teamwork requires the closest cooperation between writer, director and actor, but there is no permanent company, off-West End or off anywhere, through which to graduate as a player or a playwright.

But even after having tried out a funny idea, who is prepared to go back to the drawing board, add or remove characters or entire scenes, or completely change the plot, in order to calibrate the meticulous escalation of lunacy that takes farce into the realm of delirium?

Molière more than likely re-jigged his scripts, and we know that Ben Travers at the Aldwych and Brian Rix's Whitehall writers constantly made radical changes, even after plays had officially opened. Rix once revealed that not more than twenty minutes of the original script for *Simple Spymen* remained in the final production. Old skool writer, Ray Cooney, continues to impose huge demands on himself in order to get perfect laughs. Given the colossal creative pressures, perhaps it's no wonder that any writer or actor under thirty with even a sliver of farce in their funny bone now heads straight for television, radio or film.

Meanwhile, comedy itself is changing, the diversity of comedians and types of comedy reflecting the diversity in audiences. Stand-up is big business. Comedy is everywhere. Britain is no longer a nation of shopkeepers but a nation of comedy clubbers. Laughter tracks are in; genuine laughter is out. Observational comedy is in; joke-based comedy is out. In-yer-face verbals are in; double entendres are out. Rude is in; risqué is out. Offensive is in; inoffensive is out.

'One *must* surprise an audience out of its expectations,' Joe Orton told *Plays and Players* magazine just after *Loot* had opened in the West End in 1966, two years before the abolition of theatre censorship in England. Not surprisingly, when he was doing his utmost to shock audiences out of their moral rut by getting riotous farcical comedy out of a corpse, sexual deviation, corrupt policemen and the Catholic Church, Orton had plenty of close run-ins with the censor. But like all of the great farce writers before him, the trick was to find ways to subvert the prevailing moral codes through all those traditional farcical contraptions of artful ambiguity, wicked wit, dodgy double meanings and innocent innuendo – all the comedy contraptions that are now no longer 'in'.

Ben Travers was writing Aldwych farces when sex was even more a mortal sin than it was in the 1960s. As he recalled in a 1975 interview, 'The whole basis, the motive for everything, was that the characters wanted to go to bed with each other. People had the idea that because the censor objected to it, the public would object to it, which was a false idea. People love to have a near the knuckle laugh.'

Apart from the mirthless politically correct brigade and dangerous religious neo-Nazis, nobody wants censorship to return. Even so, farce only truly thrives on a certain kind of edgy nervous tension between the forbidden and the funny – on taking the audience very near to the knuckle, yet not near enough to knock them senseless.

Over the centuries, farceurs have sought ever more innovative ways to flex their knuckles and subvert the prevailing social, personal and moral rules, sexual or otherwise. What hope is there for the wannabe twenty-first-century farceur when the required skills are fading fast, when there are no limits to comedy, when there are no rules to subvert, when witty innuendo has been replaced by expletives, or when the neurotic desire to shock and awe an audience into laughter becomes far more important to today's so-called 'edgy' comedy establishment than comedy itself.

British farce may not be at its wits' end. But it's getting pretty close.

8. Fifty Farces to See Before You Die Laughing

A Cuckoo in the Nest (1925) Risqué comedy of misunderstandings, in which a married man and a married woman, who used to be engaged to each other, must share the same room for a night. Ben Travers adapted his 1922 novel as a gap-filler for the Aldwych Theatre team, which already had a smash hit with *Tons of Money*. Travers said he wrote it 'as a comment, in jaunty form, on the state of the divorce law, which said that any unmarried couple who spent a night together in an hotel must, incontestably, be guilty of adultery.' Catch the 1933 film version, which is virtually a record of the original stage production, to see the Aldwych farceurs in action.

A Fish Called Wanda (1988) No wonder this 'tale of murder, lust, greed, revenge, and seafood' is one of the funniest British films of all time: John Cleese wrote the script and directed alongside Ealing Comedies veteran Charles Crichton. Cleese has acknowledged a debt to the great French farceurs: 'There was a time when I used to go to the National Theatre regularly, and they would do very, very good French farces, particularly Feydeau, and I just admired them hugely, because they were wonderfully funny. First, the emotions in farce are more intense than they are in ordinary comedy, and the result is that there's more energy, and therefore bigger laughs at stake. When you combine that with the intellectual perfection of the clockwork, it's profoundly satisfying.'

A Flea in Her Ear (1907) Georges Feydeau at the height of his farcical powers. Hellishly cruel comedy, funny foreigners, speech impediments, mistaken identities, revolving beds, rampaging husbands, lusty servants, mayhem, misunderstandings – plus a good deal of hopping in and out of the sheets at the appropriately named Hotel Coq d'Or. John Mortimer's adaptation for the National Theatre production in 1966, directed by the Comédie-Française's Jacques Charon, is still the benchmark English translation. Mortimer's ubiquitous definition of farce aptly sums up the entanglements of Feydeau's adulterous and avaricious worthies in *fin-de-siècle* Paris as 'tragedy played at a thousand revolutions per minute'. Rex Harrison and Rosemary Harris starred in the 1968 film, also directed by Charon. It's not funny for one minute.

A Funny Thing Happened on the Way to the Forum (1962) Plautus-inspired musical romp woven around an inspired score by Stephen Sondheim and hilarious book by Burt Shevelove and Larry Gelbart proves that music and farce can go together, like comedy and tragedy. A right Roman laugh-a-thon.

An Italian Straw Hat (1851) Eugène Labiche and Marc Michel's surrealist nightmare. A missing hat, a lady's honour at stake, a bewildered wedding-party in pursuit, an endless stream of comic misunderstandings... Many comedians and directors have acknowledged their debt to Labiche, including Charlie Chaplin, Stan Laurel, Jacques Tati and Jerry Lewis. The 1927 silent movie version directed by René Clair is a film comedy classic. Also adapted as a musical and a ballet.

The Bear (1888) Chekhov's early short plays are based on his stories, succinct little one-act farces, or 'Vaudevilles', with a typical tragi-comic feel to them.

The Bed Before Yesterday (1976) Shortly before his 90th birthday, Ben Travers revisited farce and became a Seventies swinger with this sex comedy minus the double meaning and innocent innuendo of his earlier work. Rarely revived.

Bedroom Farce (1975) Alan Ayckbourn in typical farcical mode at a housewarming party, where four married couples who are at different stages in their relationships find their lives intersect over the course of a chaotic evening.

Black Comedy (1965) Ingenious groundbreaking one-act farce by Peter Shaffer. A fuse blows, but the blackout effect is reversed. The actors think they are in the dark, but the action is seen in full-on white light, so the audience sees them bumping into the furniture.

Boeing-Boeing (1962) Marc Camoletti's sexy air-hostess farce requires no less than seven doors, three fiancées and at least three different overnight airline bags. 'It's geometrical,' says the philandering Bernard, explaining the way he organises his love life by airline timetables, 'so precise as to be almost poetic.' The same can be said of Camoletti's stratospheric script. Full of sexy goings-on in a French farmhouse, Camoletti's *Don't Dress For Dinner* (1987) is the sequel to *Boeing-Boeing* – and it's just as funny-funny.

Box and Cox (1847) John Maddison Morton was the Eric Sykes of mid-Victorian Britain, writing genuinely popular comedy, often with a surreal edge. This one-act farce is one of his finest and most performed. In 1928 it became the first complete play to be televised by the BBC. See also Morton's *A Most Unwarrantable Intrusion* (1849), an artfully conceived one-act 'Comic Interlude' in which Mr Snoozle arranges a day at home to himself only to find his cozy Victorian world turned topsy turvy by a mad interloper. Goonery of the first order.

Can't Pay? Won't Pay! (1974) Dario Fo, a Nobel Prize winner and Italy's most celebrated comic playwright and performer, depicts what happens when people refuse to pay spiralling prices in the shops, a kind of fast and furious supermarket sweep avoiding the checkout. New productions are encouraged to update the puns and parody with topical themes and improvisations. Fo's left field brand of populist farcical comedy owes much to the traditions of the *commedia dell'arte*, circus, jesters, minstrels and political clowns.

Charley's Aunt (1892) Lord Fancourt Babberley impersonates Charley's aunt from Brazil in this hardy perennial of farce. The 'aunt', of course, behaves outrageously, smoking cigars and pouring tea into old Mr Spettigue's hat. It's been a great role for generations of comedians, the most memorable being Griff Rhys Jones, who won an Olivier Award for it in 1984. Jack Benny starred in the 1941 film version. Arthur Askey wore the frock in *Charley's (Big-Hearted) Aunt* in 1940. In a 1969 television adaptation, Danny La Rue was so convincing as the aunt that he entirely blunted the comic point. The musical adaptation, *Where's Charley*, is rarely ever staged professionally, but Auntie herself has never retired from the boards.

Chase Me, Comrade! (1964) A Russian ballet dancer defects to the West, triggering an hilarious game of hide-and-seek in which everybody is pretending to be everybody else. This brilliantly constructed Ray Cooney laughter-fest was a tour-de-farce for Brian Rix who spent most of his time onstage going through increasingly desperate disguises, including a naval officer, a ballet dancer, a ten-foot man and a talking tiger-skin. The last of the original Whitehall farces. Still performable. Somebody should revive it.

The Comedy of Errors. Double trouble in Shakespeare's homage to the Roman comedies of Plautus. See also *A Funny Thing Happened on the Way to the Forum* and listen to Rodgers and Hart's musicalisation, *The Boys from Syracuse*.

The Court Jester (1956) Danny Kaye stars in the Python-esque story of 'how the destiny of a nation was changed by a royal birthmark on the royal backside of a royal infant child.' Melvin Frank and Norman Panama's witty screenplay is packed with verbal buffoonery, including the iconic comic routine 'The pellet with the poison's in the vessel with the pestle; the chalice from the palace has the brew that is true! Right?'

Dad's Army (1968-1977) Jimmy Perry and David Croft's scripts for the Walmington-on-Sea platoon of the Home Guard commanded by pompous Captain Mainwaring are full of inspired farcical situations. See

Episode 56, in which Mainwaring's platoon is detailed to guard a captured U-Boat captain and crew.

Dry Rot (1954) John Chapman's rollicking post-war comedy about bent bookmakers switching race-horses involves heads popping unexpectedly from secret doors and falling trousers a-plenty. The second of the Whitehall farces, it's one of the very few farces in the National Theatre's *NT2000* list of significant twentieth-century plays.

She's Done It Again (1969) The very best of three anarchic farces written by Michael Pertwee for Brian Rix, it involves a financial scandal and multiple preg-nancies. The great Harold Hobson praised its 'delicious and delirious qualities'. Pertwee followed up with the equally inventive *Don't Just Lie There, Say Something* and *A Bit Between the Teeth*.

Donkey's Years (1976) Michael Frayn's university reunion comedy turns into a classic bedroom farce involving a cabinet minister. A precursor to Frayn's love letter to farce, *Noises Off*.

Duck Soup (1933) The Marx Brothers produced a lot of movies and one comedy masterpiece. This is it.

Fawlty Towers (1975 and 1979) Only two series and twelve episodes, but the cleverly plotted and superbly choreographed comic complications endured by Basil, Sybil, Manuel and co (and their creators John Cleese and Connie Booth) showed how farce on television can fit perfectly into the traditions of the very best on stage.

Frasier (1993-2004) Writer Joe Keenan must have had Feydeau in mind when he wrote 'The Ski Lodge' episode of *Frasier* in which Frasier, Niles and the family become embroiled in what turns into a helter-skelter bedroom farce. But then the entire series maintained farce at its heart.

The Frogs (405 BC) Aristophanes had plenty to croak about in his day, but this Athenian entertainer's comedies are infrequently performed today.

The Front Page (1928) Probably the best American farce of the 1920s, in which Charles MacArthur and Ben Hecht take satirical sideswipes at a pack of scheming journalists and big city corruption. In fact it was so good they filmed it thrice, the 1940 Howard Hawks version re-titled as *His Girl Friday*.

Government Inspector (2011) David Harrower's new version of the Gogol masterpiece, directed by Richard Jones for the Young Vic, deleted the 'The' from the original title and turned a small-town satire into a full-strength Vodka-fuelled hallucinatory farce teetering on the brink of insanity.

I Love Lucy (1951-1957) Time and time again the all-time comedy genius that was Lucille Ball gets herself embroiled in farcical situations in one of the greatest sitcoms ever to come out of American television.

The Importance of Being Earnest (1895) With a handbag bulging with clever lines, puns, epigrams and repartees, Oscar Wilde employed farce as a façade for poking fun at Victorian values. A work of genius.

The Ladies Man (1961) Hardly any nutty gurning here from Jerry Lewis as the handyman at a ladies-only boarding house, but lots of superb slow-burn film comedy, inventive sight gags and farcical set-piece routines, culminating in a ballroom dance with a grim-faced George Raft.

Lend Me A Tenor (1986) Ken Ludwig's backstage farce brings chaos, double entendres, scantily clad young women and zany mayhem to the world of provincial opera. A musical adaptation slowed down the farcical comedy but musically hit the right notes.

La Cage aux Folles (1973) Rediscover Jean Poiret's original play about what happens when a drag queen and his night club-owning 'husband' cover up their relationship to try and appear respectable. It spawned the gloriously funny film, two not quite so funny sequels, a mediocre Hollywood remake and the brilliant stage musical.

Le Dîner de Cons (1998) Superb movie version of Francis Veber's 1993 smash-hit farce, in which a group of urbane Parisians amuse themselves by inviting a series of nerds to dinner. Ronald Harwood translated the original play in 2002, re-titled *See You Next Tuesday*, but it was no match for the film.

Let's Get a Divorce (1880) Victorien Sardou was a successful French dramatist, though his well-made plays are seldom performed any more. Bernard Shaw coined the word 'Sardoodledom' to describe them. This one flirts like mad with the marriage-go-round and is still perky enough to be revisited.

Loot (1965) Joe Orton's first real attempt at farce started out on tour as a disaster but eventually ended up as a successful tour-de-force of bad taste brilliance and funereal humour. Unhappy with the original cast and direction, Orton wrote to his producer 'Ideally, it should be nearer *The Homecoming* than *I Love Lucy*. Don't think I'm a snob about *I Love Lucy*. I've watched it often. I think it's very funny. But it's aimed purely at making an audience laugh. And that isn't the prime aim of *Loot*.'

The Magistrate (1885) Arthur Wing Pinero's nimble plot tilts at Victorian values by sending a compromised Establishment figure – a nice old metropolitan magistrate – through a moral mangle after he unwittingly visits a dubious hotel.

Noises Off (1982) The double whammy farce-inside-a-farce by Michael Frayn where offstage is even crazier than onstage and backstage is full of back-stabbing actors and stage managers. Done with the right level energy, it's a riotous celebration of the old showbiz adage that come what may, 'the show must go on'. The play premiered in 1982, but Frayn has since rewritten it several times.

No Sex Please, We're British (1971) As if to prove there is a wall of cultural snobbery built around popular farce, Alistair Foot and Anthony Marriott's cracking comedy about an ordinary young couple caught up in a pornography scandal was panned by the critics but ran and ran in the West End.

One for the Pot (1956) This top-notch Ray Cooney and Tony Hilton laughter machine is still a Rolls-Royce of farces, involving an inheritance claim and a seemingly endless tangle of mistaken identities and hilarious confusions.

One Man, Two Guvnors (2011) Farcicality and the *commedia dell'arte* conventions are constantly popping up in Richard Bean's ingenious 1960s reworking of Goldoni's *The Servant of Two Masters*, complete with a doddery old servant and a frenzied slapstick food-serving scene.

Potiche (2010) French farce is very much alive and kicking in French movies, as in this staggeringly sophisticated and extremely funny film from director François Ozon, based on a 1980 stage farce by Pierre Barillet and Jean-Pierre Grédy, with Catherine Deneuve as a *potiche,* or trophy wife, who rebels against her hubbie.

The Pot of Gold (195BC) Titus Maccius Plautus wasn't to know that his one-act sitcoms would become the template for broad farcical comedy thereafter, from Shakespeare to the *commedia dell'arte* and beyond. *The Pot of Gold* became Molière's *The Miser.*

The Producers (2001) Mel Brooks reckons the musical version of his 1968 film is 'an old-fashioned, traditional musical comedy.' It's also a musical farce to reckon with.

Run For Your Wife (1982) A bigamist taxi driver's nightmare of lies and deception spirals into the ultimate Ray Cooney farce.

See How They Run (1945) Various de-trousered vicars, a bishop, a dopey maid, a repressed spinster and a German POW all run riot in Philip King's typically British romp. Includes the classic farce line: 'Sergeant, arrest most of these vicars'.

Sons of the Desert (1933) Many of the Laurel and Hardy shorts employ farcical situations. Here the two chumps get themselves into another nice mess when they sneak off to a convention while pretending to their wives they are on a medicinal cruise.

Tartuffe (1664) A hypocritical fraudster masquerades as a holy man and tries to get hold of his friend's estate by sending him to jail. 'Such hypocrites are far from rare, In fact you'll find them everywhere'. Denounced as sacrilegious by the Church, Molière's biting comedy was banned from public performance by Louis XIV.

The Servant of Two Masters (1743) Has a permanent place in the catalogue of classic comedies, but someone should blow the cobwebs from Carlo Goldoni's numerous other comedies and give them a chance to make the grade too. The mirth-maker of Venice wrote some brilliant stuff. Pity we never see it performed.

Some Like It Hot (1959) 'Nobody's perfect', as the ending goes, and nobody can deny that Billy Wilder and A.L. Diamond created the perfect film farce.

What the Butler Saw (1969) A mad psychoanalyst instructs his new secretary to undress, triggering off a chain of inspired farcical invention and Orton-esque verve and verbosity. Joe Orton's biographer John Lahr calls this play Orton's farce masterpiece. 'Orton made comedy out of the ideas behind the farce form. Where Orton's earlier plays had lacked the scenic surprise to match the jolt of the lines, Orton was now using the stage with an inventiveness no modern comic playwright had dared.' By the time it opened in 1969 stage censorship had been abolished but some of Orton's bare-faced cheek was still edited out, including Winston Churchill's phallus, which became a cigar.

Yes, Prime Minister (2010) In Antony Jay and Jonathan Lynn's clever stage adaptation of their hit TV series, Jim Hacker and Sir Humphrey Appleby get themselves into a farcical frenzy dealing with the consequences of an oil crisis, political blackmail, an underage sex scandal and the media spinning out of their control.

Bibliography of sources

Barber, C.L. (1959), *Shakespeare's Festive Comedy*. Princeton, N.J.: Princeton University Press

Bentley, Eric (1958), *Let's Get a Divorce! and Other Plays*. (New York: Hill and Wang

Booth, M.R. (1973) (ed.), *English Plays in the 19th Century*, vol. IV. Oxford: Clarendon Press

Brown, Ivor (1955), *Theatre 1954-5*. London: Max Reinhardt

Davis, Jessica Milner Davis (1978), *Farce*. London: Methuen

Frayn, Michael (1992), *Plays: 2*. London: Methuen Drama

Gelbart, Larry (1998), *Laughing Matters: On Writing Mash, Tootsie, Oh, God!, and a Few Other Funny Things*. New York: Random House

Griffin, Peter (2005), *Ken Dodd: The Biography*. London: Michael O'Mara Books

Hartnoll, Phyllis and Found, Peter (1996) (eds.), *The Concise Oxford Companion to the Theatre*. Oxford: Oxford University Press

Hughes, Leo (1956), *A Century of English Farce*. Princeton, N.J.: Princeton University Press

Kerr, Walter (1968), *Tragedy and Comedy*. London: The Bodley Head

Lahr, John (1976), *Orton: The Complete Plays*, Introduction. London: Eyre Methuen

McCann, Graham (2007), *Fawlty Towers*. London: Hodder & Stoughton

Nathan, David (1971), *The Laughtermakers: Quest for Comedy*. London: Peter Owen

Rix, Brian (1975), *My Farce From My Elbow*. London: Secker & Warburg

Rix, Brian (1989), *Farce About Face*. London: Hodder & Stoughton

Russell Taylor, John (1967), *The Rise and Fall of the Well-Made Play*. London: Methuen

Shapiro, Norman R. (1959) (ed. and introduction), *Four Farces – Georges Feydeau*. New York: Applause

Simpson, Harold (1930), *Excursions in Farce*. London: Besant & Co.

Smith, Leslie (1989), *Modern British Farce*. London: Macmillan

Tanitch, Robert (2007), *London Stage in the 20th Century*. London: Haus Publishing

Tanitch, Robert (2010), *London Stage in the Nineteenth Century*. Lancaster: Carnegie Publishing

Travers, Ben (1957), *Vale of Laughter*. London: Geoffrey Bles

Trussler, Simon (1966), 'Farce' in *Plays and Players* (June 1966).

Wilde, Larry (2000), *Great Comedians Talk about Comedy*. New York: Executive Books/Jester Press

Wilmut, Roger (1985), *Kindly Leave the Stage – The Story of Variety, 1919-60*. London: Methuen

www.ingramcontent.com/pod-product-compliance
Ingram Content Group UK Ltd.
Pitfield, Milton Keynes, MK11 3LW, UK
UKHW020453060325
455687UK00014B/68

9 781849 431514